RULES OF THUMB FOR RESEARCH

JAY SILVERMAN
Nassau Community College

ELAINE HUGHES
Nassau Community College

DIANA ROBERTS WIENBROER
Nassau Community College

Boston, MA   Burr Ridge, IL   Dubuque, IA   Madison, WI
New York, NY   San Francisco, CA   St. Louis, MO
Bangkok   Bogotá   Caracas   Lisbon   London   Madrid   Mexico City
Milan   New Delhi   Seoul   Singapore   Sydney   Taipei   Toronto

McGraw-Hill College

A Division of The **McGraw·Hill** Companies

1 2 3 4 5 6 7 8 9 0 DOC/DOC 9 0 9 8 7 6 5 4 3 2 1 0 9

ISBN 0–07–236331–2

Editorial Director: *Phillip A. Butcher*
Senior Sponsoring Editor: *Lisa Moore*
Developmental Editor: *Emily Sparano*
Project Manager: *Christine Parker*
Production Supervisor: *Michael McCormick*
Designer: *Kiera Cunningham* and *Pam Verros*
Compositor: *Shepherd, Inc.*
Typeface: *11/13 Palatino*
Printer: *R. R. Donnelley & Sons Company*

The Library of Congress has catalogued an earlier version of this book as follows:

Silverman, Jay (date)
    Rules of thumb for research / Jay Silverman, Elaine Hughes, Diana
Roberts Wienbroer. — 1st ed.
        p.   cm.
    Includes index.
    ISBN 0–07–027639–0 (alk. paper)
    1. Report writing—Handbooks, manuals, etc.   2. Research—
Handbooks, manuals, etc.   3. Academic writing—Handbooks, manuals,
etc.   I. Hughes, Elaine.   II. Wienbroer, Diana Roberts.
III. Title.
LB2369.S52
808′.02—dc21   98–7629

http://www.mhhe.com/writers

DEDICATION

To all of our students—past, present, and future
To Tim Julet—our superb editor

■ ACKNOWLEDGMENTS

Many friends and colleagues have contributed to
Rules of Thumb for Research.

First, we wish to thank Tim Julet, our editor at McGraw-Hill, who
believed in this project, provided detailed editorial support, and
guided it through many difficult passages. Also at McGraw-Hill,
Alan Joyce and Christine Parker have been both skillful and helpful
in solving a variety of problems; Kiera Cunningham gave us an
elegant design; and Jane Morgan of Shepherd, Inc., has been the
ideal compositor. On a special note, we also wish to thank Patricia
Rossi.

As always, our students at Nassau Community College have
assisted us in our attempt to meet their needs. In particular, Diana
Wienbroer's English 101 NB (Fall 1997) and 101 NA (Spring 1998)
used and evaluated large portions of our manuscript.

A number of colleagues have thoughtfully reviewed *Rules of Thumb
for Research:* Jane Collins, Pace University; Jerome Garger, Lane
Community College; Elaine Horne, Manchester Community-
Technical College; Margaret Sabol, Cuyahoga Community College;
Polly Marshall, Hinds Community College; William A. Nagle,
Middlesex Community-Technical College; and Gian Pagnucci,
Indiana University of Pennsylvania. We are grateful for their careful
attention to every aspect of our book.

Finally, we want to thank our families—Beverly Jensen, for many
kinds of support; Carl and Kirtley Wienbroer, for design and
research advice.

Portions of *Rules of Thumb for Research* have appeared in different forms in *Rules of
Thumb: A Guide for Writers, Good Measures: A Practice Book to Accompany Rules of
Thumb, The McGraw-Hill Guide to Electronic Research* (all from McGraw-Hill), and
Finding Answers: A Guide to Conducting and Reporting Research (HarperCollins).

CONTENTS

PART 1: FIRST STEPS

PART 2: BECOMING A TRUE RESEARCHER

PART 5: DOCUMENTATION: GIVING CREDIT TO YOUR SOURCES

Part 6: Finishing Your Paper

Epilogue: Going Further

Appendix

Index

About the Authors

PREFACE
RESEARCH GIVES YOU POWER

Research can give you power—the power to get what you want. Taking the time to do even a little research can give you the edge in most situations, such as a job search, a legal fight, or a car purchase. In fact, the ability to conduct research can affect your entire life and perhaps even save your life.

Think, for example, of how people react when they have a serious injury or illness. Too often they become passive and put themselves into a doctor's hands without asking important questions. But if you have the habits and skills of research, you can take a much more active role in your recovery and approach your problem in an informed way. The results could make a crucial difference in how fully and quickly you recover.

Or if making money is your concern, research can show you the way to personal wealth. To invest successfully you must first develop keen research skills. The same is true for starting your own business: the research that you do ahead of time can make the difference between success or failure.

We wrote *Rules of Thumb for Research* to serve as a bridge between academic research and personal research, the kind of research you do for a required paper and the kind of spontaneous research you do when you have to make decisions that affect the course of your life. Learning to conduct research, which often begins with a single term paper, can ultimately become a way of life for you—for the rest of your life.

A Note from the Authors

The phrase *rule of thumb* refers to a handy guideline: The top part of your thumb is roughly an inch long. Sometimes you need a ruler, marked in millimeters, but often you can do fine by measuring with just your thumb. Your thumb takes only a second to use, and it's always with you. We wrote our first book, *Rules of Thumb: A Guide for Writers*, to create a handbook students could use on their own—brief and readable, covering the main writing problems that today's students have trouble with.

We've aimed to make *Rules of Thumb for Research* the same sort of book. You can use it out of order, in small doses, to find what you want when you need to solve a specific problem; or you can use it as a step-by-step guide to writing a research paper.

In this book you will find some points that have to be exactly right, and in those cases we've given the complete details. But where we could, we've given you a rule of thumb—a brief guide that you can quickly use any time you need to write a research paper.

PART 1

FIRST STEPS

CHAPTER 1

Before You Plunge In

(A Few Tricks of the Trade)

You may already be raring to get started on your paper. But even if you know something about doing research, stop and reflect on these six good ideas that can save you time and prevent frustration.

▪ Begin Writing from the Start

Although you may think you can't begin writing until you've done a lot of research, you can begin discovering and defining your own view of the topic before you even set foot in the library.

Trick of the trade: **Begin writing early and keep writing all during the process.** Start a section in your notebook where you jot down your ideas, make lists, and write bits or pieces that might go into your paper. Make it a habit to write at every step. Then you will already have parts of your paper written before you even sit down to write it.

▪ Learn to Use Computers

Using computers is now a basic skill expected of all college students. Computers are essential in helping you produce a research paper. They enable you to edit and re-edit, move blocks of information, add graphics and design, and print out a professional-looking paper. Computer programs will count your words for you, check your spelling and grammar, and store each new version you write.

Trick of the trade: **Get the help that you need.** If you don't already know how to type or aren't familiar with the basics of computer use, enroll in a beginner's class immediately. If you have limited experience with using computers, go to the college computer lab for practice and assistance. Chapter 10 of this book, "Researching on Computers," can help you get started.

☐ Explore Different Avenues of Research

You probably already have a preference for the kinds of materials you like to use. You might find it easy to search the Internet and difficult to go to the library. Or you might know how to find a book in the library but not how to find articles in periodicals. Or you might enjoy getting articles from magazines at home but don't like reading newspapers on microfilm. Don't limit your research by sticking only to the avenues you're most comfortable with.

Trick of the trade: **When gathering information, go beyond books, encyclopedias, and popular magazines.** Look for journals devoted to special studies, brochures, old clippings, local histories, and so forth. Deliberately search for sources outside the library: conduct interviews or surveys, use the Internet, visit nearby museums and institutions, listen to the radio and watch TV to gather up-to-the-minute information on your topic. Chapter 13 of this book, "Sleuthing for Valuable Resources," will give you many other research ideas.

☐ Keep a Record of Your Sources of Information

Your final research paper will require *documentation*, a prescribed system for identifying your sources of information. You will need to report the specific pages where you found information, as well as the authors, titles, and publishing data of the sources you use. It's possible to write a very good paper and still get a failing grade because you did not pay attention to the details of documentation. Therefore, as you conduct your research, be sure to record the necessary information for each source you use.

Trick of the trade: **Write a notecard for each source of information that you consult.** Make a practice of filling out a card for every source, even those you doubt you'll use. You never know when you might need to check or refer to the source at a later date. Each notecard should contain information that allows you to find the source again. Such information usually includes the name of the author or speaker, the title (book, article, radio show, etc.), the date of publication, place and publisher, and page numbers. You can label each card with the type of source it is as a way to remind yourself to use a variety of sources. Part 5 of this book gives you the details you need to correctly document your sources.

◼ KNOW HOW TO START

Getting started is usually a very personal, sometimes quirky, choice. Some people have to sharpen every pencil in the house. Others have to lounge on the sofa and daydream awhile. Still others can't start working until they have a stack of books and a lot of snacks spread out on the desk. The only start you absolutely want to avoid is deciding ahead of time exactly what your paper will say even before you begin your research. Taking all the surprise and challenge out of the search will guarantee you a pretty dull adventure—and paper.

Trick of the trade: **To get a sense of the general process for the whole project, look over the Table of Contents for this book.** The sequence of the chapters will give you a step-by-step idea of how to go about producing a research paper. You can, however, start with the chapter that appeals to you most. Start in the middle if that's what will get you moving. If you usually procrastinate, you might first read the six "In a Crunch" chapters which end each part.

◼ KNOW WHEN TO STOP

A major decision all researchers face is gauging how much time to allow for the research and how much time to allow for writing the finished paper. Writing the paper will almost always take much longer than you expect, so be sure to write parts of it as you go along. That way you can discover gaps in your information while you still have time to do some more research. The biggest pitfall, however, is continuing to do research far beyond what is useful for your paper and then shortchanging your time to edit and refine.

Trick of the trade: **Set a deadline for your research.** To keep from falling into a bottomless research hole, set a reasonable date by which you plan to have completed your research—and stick to that date as closely as possible. This date should ideally be a week before your final paper is due to allow time for writing, editing, filling in gaps, and producing a correct and readable paper.

CHAPTER 2

BRAINSTORMING

(TO FIND A TOPIC YOU CARE ABOUT)

■ WHAT IT IS

When you brainstorm, you have a problem or question in mind—something puzzling that you want to solve. You give yourself a period of time—say twenty minutes—and you very rapidly list any ideas that come to you, jotting down just a word or phrase as each idea comes. As you brainstorm:

- Make a number of lists rapidly.

- Stick with one subject and go over it several times.

- Push on and continue to brainstorm even after you think you've run dry.

- Draw the connection between ideas with diagrams, sketches, clusters, and so forth.

Brainstorming is not a waste of time. Brainstorming needs unhurried time. Yet most students are in a hurry and want to get to the library, line up some sources, and start writing. To them, brainstorming sounds like delay and unnecessary work. In fact, the opposite is true: Taking time now to brainstorm will save you much more time later because you will proceed with a clear sense of the project. You will go to the library with specific questions and ideas in mind.

Creation often begins with chaos. Brainstorming is by its nature chaotic, so it may seem uncomfortable to you at first because you aren't always in control of what your brain gives you. But don't let the onslaught of ideas and questions overwhelm you. If you keep pushing through, you'll be rewarded with better ideas than you could have discovered through a totally controlled approach.

◼ A TECHNIQUE FOR BRAINSTORMING

Here's a method for brainstorming you can use to uncover many different topics that have something to do with your life and goals. If you are free to choose your own topic for a paper, make it one you feel passionate about. The choices are endless. The topic can be a field you have studied in school; it can relate to your future career; it can be some offbeat subject you've always wanted to know about; or it can be a subject that will improve your life in some way.

Any topic can become a subject for serious research. The topic is less important than your wholehearted desire to study the subject inside and out, to live with it until you become an expert on the topic and can share your knowledge with others.

In a notebook, put each of the following questions on a separate page:

- What possible topics do I already have experience in?
- What topics do I want to know more about?
- What goals do I have in life right now?
- What challenges and problems do I face right now?

List as many items as possible under each question. Keep going until you get at least ten under each of the four questions.

Circle the one item on each of the four lists that feels most important to you right now. In other words, from each list, you choose one topic and then you will brainstorm that particular topic again.

On the back of each page, put the topic you circled at the top. Under it

- List everything you already know about the topic.
- List everything you'd like to find out about the topic.

Continue until you've done all four lists. From each of your new lists, choose one possible research topic. When you've finished, you should have four very specific topics that are of interest to you.

■ If You Get Stuck

If, after brainstorming, your lists are too short or you've ended up with blank pages, here's a quick method that might unstick you.

- Write a list of everything you did or thought yesterday.
- Or write a list of everything you love (or hate).
- Or make a list of the most pressing questions you have about your life.

These lists should be easy to make and will get you shifted into the list-making mode.

If you're still bogged down, ask a friend to look over your lists and discuss some possibilities with you. Or simply talking over your ideas with someone else may get you going.

CHAPTER 3

FREEWRITING

(TO FIND A TOPIC YOU CARE ABOUT)

■ WHAT IT IS

When you freewrite, you write without any of the usual constraints, such as correctness and coherence. You write for a preset time, usually ten to twenty minutes, and you write rapidly without stopping to make any corrections. At its best, freewriting is a lot like talking to yourself. When you freewrite,

- Write whatever comes to mind even if it doesn't seem to make sense.

- Write nonstop without lifting your pen from the paper.

- Push yourself to keep writing until the set time is completely up.

Freewriting is not a waste of time. In fact, freewriting can often lead you to your best ideas. Freewriting gives you a shortcut to these ideas and gets you past your first reactions to the topic. Twenty minutes of freewriting early in a project can save you hours of writing in circles because it will lead you to your "home" in the topic—that is, the area where you feel most comfortable and inspired.

Freewriting, like brainstorming, is a chaotic, creative process. It takes some practice to train yourself to write rapidly, nonstop, and without thinking things out ahead of time. When you freewrite, you free up the writer in you instead of censoring your ideas before they even get down on paper.

■ A TECHNIQUE FOR FREEWRITING

Brainstorming is best used when you are searching for a topic, whereas freewriting is best used when you already have a general topic in mind. The two activities can, in fact, often be used together, first brainstorming to find a topic and then freewriting to find your particular interest in the topic.

Once you select a topic you care about, you might initially feel that you don't know enough to write anything about it without doing some prior reading or research. This is seldom the case. You are usually much better off doing at least one freewrite, perhaps even two, before you start looking outside yourself for information. These initial writings will nearly always surprise you with the amount of information you already know and they are also invaluable in helping you discover your own point of view toward the topic.

Set a Time Limit

Set aside ten to twenty minutes by the clock and begin freewriting. Put your topic at the top of the page. Keep writing until the time is up, no matter what. The best material often comes right at the point when you think you've exhausted everything you have to say.

Keep Your Pen Moving

Write rapidly. Don't stop to think, to check spelling, to reread, or to evaluate what you're writing. Make yourself write as quickly and as continuously as you possibly can. If your mind goes blank, write a simple word such as *and* over and over until a new thought comes to you.

Read What You've Written Only After Your Time Is Up

Don't go back and read over what you've written until your time is completely up. Then read what you've written with an open mind. Don't begin editing or correcting yet. Mark any spot that surprises or excites you.

◼ If You Get Stuck

If you are still facing a blank page at the end of your freewriting and can't seem to get your hand moving, here are some ideas that might get your writing underway:

- Make a list of three or four questions related to your topic. What are some of the gaps in your knowledge of this subject or things you'd like to find out more about? Use one of the questions and write out an answer off the top of your head. It doesn't have to be accurate or make sense.

- Write about why you feel stuck. What seems to interfere between you and the writing in this very moment?

- Write everything you know about the topic, even if it seems minor or superficial.

- Find an informative paragraph about your topic and copy it down slowly, taking in the details as you write. Then freewrite about what you just copied.

If you're still staring at a blank piece of paper, find someone to talk with until you gain some inspiration or a new idea.

CHAPTER 4

When You Face a "Boring" Topic

(Finding Yourself a Home in Any Topic)

There's no escaping those assigned topics you will meet up with in just about every kind of academic course. The trick is to find some little corner of any subject—from "How Fleas Jump" to "The Influence of Henry George on Economics"—that you can call *home*. If you have to do research on a topic not of your choosing, you can at least choose to be interested in one particular area. For example, if the politics of Tammany Hall bores you, you might investigate how corruption affected families like yours during that era.

◼ No Subject Is a Total Waste of Time

No subject is truly a waste of time, and every subject has something interesting about it. Search for some aspect of the subject that is real to you by listing several possible answers to each of the following three questions:

- How does the subject tie in with any present concerns about my life?

- How does it relate to issues I have thought about in the past?

- In what ways might this subject be important to me later in life?

Let's suppose you have been assigned a very remote topic such as "The Gods of Mesopotamia." Here is a religion that no one has believed in for two thousand years. What in this subject can possibly matter to you? Let's say that your biggest concern right now is getting married. Can you tie the topic of Mesopotamian gods to how the Mesopotamians viewed marriage and how they conducted courtship and weddings?

In other words, find one aspect of any subject that you can relate to some part of your own life, either your present, past, or future.

☐ BRAINSTORMING WHEN YOU HAVE AN ASSIGNED TOPIC

Brainstorming is useful for narrowing down a wide subject to a very specific one.

- Put the subject at the top of the page.
- Make a list of every subtopic you can think of. Include all the authors, facts, historical background, and so forth that you have studied.
- Make a list of everything you already know about the subject.
- Make a list of other things you would like to find out about.
- Go back and circle three of the subjects that interest you most.
- Put each of these three topics on a separate page and brainstorm each.
- Choose the one that either excites you the most or the one you feel most competent about.

You may find you have more questions on your list than you do topics you know something about. That's fine. A question that interests you can be the start of an intriguing research project.

☐ FREEWRITING WHEN YOU HAVE AN ASSIGNED TOPIC

Freewriting will help you to find your own angle in any topic, and it's especially helpful when you've been assigned a very specific one. Writing in a totally informal way will coax out some attitude, opinion, or question about even the remotest subject.

- Put the topic at the top of a blank page.
- Set the clock for twenty minutes.

- Begin writing rapidly without paying any attention to correctness or coherence.

- Keep your pen moving and don't stop until the twenty minutes are up.

- Write briefly about any associations you already have with the topic, no matter how unrelated they might seem at first.

- Write also about any questions you might want answered.

- Go back and carefully read what you've written.

At the bottom of the freewrite, write one sentence that sums up the most important point for you. This sentence can often be used as your opening sentence or even as the thesis statement for your paper.

◼ If You're Still Stuck

Talk to someone. Sit down with a classmate, a family member, a teacher, a librarian, a tutor in the writing center. Explain your problem and go over your ideas one at a time. Be open to their suggestions, but don't depend on them to completely solve your problem. Instead, take note also of what you say, the ideas that start coming to your own mind. Make notes throughout the conversation. Then go to a quiet place and do some new brainstorming and freewriting.

CHAPTER 5

FORMULATING YOUR QUESTIONS

(FOR A DIRECT ROUTE TO YOUR DESTINATION)

The trick to doing efficient research—that is, research that doesn't cost you debilitating time and effort—is starting out with some well-formulated questions. If you have a few of them in hand before you begin your research, you can move straight ahead and avoid going in circles and wasting a lot of your valuable time. Good questions will give you a strong focus for your research.

■ GUIDELINES FOR FORMULATING GOOD QUESTIONS

Set off a section of your notebook just for questions. Add to your list any new questions that occur to you as you read, write, and research.

Go Over Your Brainstorming and Freewriting Exercises

You probably have already jotted down some questions as you did your brainstorming and freewriting. Go back and retrieve them. Rewrite them until they say exactly what you want to know. Where you may have jotted down something brief, such as "What are Stephen Crane's most famous short stories?" you might then expand to yield deeper information, such as: "What are some common elements found in Stephen Crane's most famous short stories?"

Frame Your Questions to Yield a Flow of Information

Take extra care to avoid questions that can be answered with simply a yes or no or just a few words. For example, if you are doing research on the early railroads in America, a question such as "What train lines offered the first passenger service?" will give you only a short list. A more fruitful question, which will yield a couple of paragraphs, might be: "What innovations in train travel did the Santa Fe line introduce?"

Do not list questions to which you already know the answer. Ask real and provocative questions.

Don't Be Too Easily Satisfied with Your Questions

As you get deeper into your research, keep looking for intriguing questions. Sometimes a new question can open up a whole new way of looking at your topic. Let's say you have been assigned or have chosen a topic in your American Government class on the decrease of crime in cities. Rather than going with the most obvious question, "What has caused the crime rates to drop?" you might ask yourself a provocative question, such as: "In what ways is crime in cities affected by changing economic factors?"

Relate Any Research Topic to Your Own Life

You can take any research topic and ask relevant questions about its impact on your own life, either something that used to be important to you, something that is currently important to you, or something that will be important to you at some future time.

Take, for example, that remote and potentially "boring" topic mentioned in the previous chapter, "The Gods of Mesopotamia." You've done your brainstorming and your freewriting, and you're still stumped. Take some time to look back over both, and mark at least one or two spots that you can persuade yourself to look into further. If you decide that you'd like to tie the topic into your current interest in getting married, you might come up with a couple of questions such as:

- How did religious beliefs of the Mesopotamians influence their decisions about choosing marriage partners?

- What direct influence did the gods exert over marriages? What were the customs, ceremonies, rules, and so forth?

With a couple of good questions such as these, you can manage to turn a bland topic into one that entices you at least a little.

■ NOW TURN YOUR QUESTIONS INTO A RESEARCH STRATEGY

Once you've settled on a focused topic through brainstorming, freewriting, and formulating questions, you're in a good position to let your questions organize your research.

- Review your questions. You should have at least three to begin with.

- Rank the questions in order of highest interest to you right now.

- Begin your research with your first question; then move progressively to the other questions as time and interest allow. You may find that your last question turns out to be the one of major interest to you after you've done some preliminary research.

- Don't hesitate to adjust, refine, or replace these questions until you find the ones that most interest you. Then keep these questions in front of you all during your research to stay on track at every stage of your project.

- Keep in mind, also, that sometimes you might come up with a single question so intriguing and full of potential that it can start you on the road to a very rewarding investigation. The more skill you gain in formulating questions, the more often you will come up with a single, fruitful question.

As you develop the skill of formulating intriguing questions for any subject you encounter, whether personal or academic, you will be building a habit of thought that can make you a lifelong researcher.

CHAPTER 6

IN A CRUNCH 1
(GETTING TO YOUR RESEARCH)

At the end of each of the six parts of *Rules of Thumb for Research* is a chapter specifically for those times when you find yourself frantically working at the eleventh hour. Whether you're a procrastinator, a perfectionist, a good researcher, or a poor one, you will find yourself every so often in a crunch.

◼ IF YOU'RE A PROCRASTINATOR

You already know you'll be frantically writing your paper up until the last minute. Be realistic about the time you actually have for research, and don't attempt to do more than you know you can get done by the deadline.

- Do not skip brainstorming, freewriting, or formulating questions no matter how pressed you are. Even an hour spent on these activities will give you a goal so you don't waste valuable time.

- Decide on a reasonable number of sources and amount of reading you can do, depending on the requirements of your project.

- Survey your sources thoroughly; analyze which sources can help you the most and go directly to those.

◼ IF YOU'RE A PERFECTIONIST

- Don't organize or outline too soon. The purpose of research is to discover what you did not expect. Leave some room for surprises in your process of researching.

- Set a deadline for your research. Normally you should stop searching for more sources approximately one week before your paper is due.

- Don't panic and rush out and do fifty extra things you really don't need to do.

☐ IF YOU'VE COME UP BLANK AND HAVE NO TOPIC

If you have a free choice of topic and have done the brainstorming, freewriting, and questions and still don't have a topic, there's hope. A quick way to get an interesting topic is to look at a problem you have observed in your own life or in your community. Chances are these problems are common to most other people and communities. Think about doing research that will help solve the problem. The big caution here is to avoid the huge and overpublicized issues. Rather than researching overfishing of the ocean, you could concentrate on what happened to your childhood fishing hole. Keep your topic small and close to home and you'll be able to do faster research.

☐ IF YOU CAN'T GET STARTED ON AN ASSIGNED TOPIC

If you find yourself stewing and unable to make a definite start, go directly to your teacher as soon as possible and tell the truth. Ask for help. A brief conversation with the teacher who assigned the topic will probably be of great benefit and inspiration. Your teacher may also be willing to give you a new slant on the topic.

☐ TAKE TIME TO FREEWRITE EVEN IF YOU'RE IN A PANIC

Once you've settled on a topic, even at this late date, you should freewrite first before you begin your research. Freewriting is seldom a waste of writing time because it will focus your research and give you direction. A freewrite can often be completely or partially incorporated right into your paper. Sometimes it can even become the heart of your paper. Freewriting also slows down the panic state and helps you focus your energies and ideas.

PART 2

Becoming a True Researcher

CHAPTER 7

WORKING WITH SUBJECT HEADINGS

(YOUR FIRST SEARCH STRATEGY)

When you look for books, articles, and other sources of information—whether using print indexes or computers—you will be looking at a list of subjects or typing in a subject. Most research is best done by using subject headings and using progressively narrower headings as you continue your search.

- In the library catalog, you can search for a specific title or author, but for most topics, you will use the *subject* catalog.

- Indexes of periodical articles, most databases, and search engines on the Internet are organized by subject.

What you find in these listings depends on what you ask for, the *headings* you look up. Learning to use subject headings is a major skill you will need as a researcher. Be flexible and persistent in trying many different subject headings to find the information you want.

■ HOW TO FIND A VARIETY OF HEADINGS FOR YOUR SUBJECT

To be successful, you will need several headings or search terms to try. Here are some strategies to gather terms you can use:

- **Begin by using your own terms from brainstorming, freewriting, and listing questions.** Prepare a list of key words that you can look up on the computer or in print. If your original words do not yield what you need, you will have to keep refining your terms until you get the ones that give you what you are looking for.

- **Expand your terms.** Look for terms in a general reference article, or in the tables of contents and indexes of books. When you find a book in the library catalog that best matches your topic, look at the subject headings listed for it in "full display" and use those for more searches.

- **Use computers.** Check the thesaurus or word list if you are using a database. Check the categories listed on Internet subject search engines (such as *Yahoo!* and *Magellan*) to find subtopics. Query search engines (such as *AltaVista* and *Webcrawler*) offer a variety of related subject headings to try; these are usually listed at the bottom of the Web sites.

◻ If You Come Up Blank

Don't quit too easily. Stay with the topic you were planning to use and keep refining your terms until you find important leads. Changing subjects in the middle of your research will nearly always confuse you and cause you to waste valuable time.

Try Synonyms

If you are looking up English attitudes toward work, you may need to look under "Great Britain" or "United Kingdom" instead of "England." You may also need to look under "labor" or "labour" instead of "work."

Consult the *Library of Congress Subject Headings* (in print or on the Internet) to be sure you're using the right words for your topic.

Try a Broader Heading

Sometimes your heading can be too narrow and you'll have to use additional terms. If you're searching for the Buick Riviera, using just "Riviera" may get you only listings about beaches on the Mediterranean Sea; try adding "Buick" or use "General Motors," and then search for "Riviera."

Try a Specialized Listing

If you are looking up a specific medication, a listing of popular magazines (such as *InfoTrak* or *The Reader's Guide to Periodical*

Literature) may give you very little. Turn instead to a specialized listing such as *Medline* on computers and *Index Medicus* in print. The Appendix in this book gives some of these specialized listings. Your librarian or a teacher can help you find others.

☐ IF YOU FIND TOO MANY SOURCES

If you keep pulling up an overwhelming number of sources with your search term, you'll need to quickly narrow it down.

Limit Your Term Further

If you want to study college courses offered on television, looking under a broad term such as "education" would give you an unmanageable number of sources. Try "educational TV" or "distance learning."

Combine Headings

On most computer databases and Internet search engines, you can type in two or more terms that will narrow your topic. If you are studying varieties of roses, just typing in "rose" might get you articles on Pete Rose or the War of the Roses. Try "roses and varieties." For instructions on using search strings, see Chapter 11, "How to Conduct a Computer Search."

Limit Your Search by Dates

When searching indexes in bound volumes, for most topics use only recent volumes. On databases you can type in a range of dates ("amnesty international 1992–1996") to control the amount of information you receive at any one time.

As you work with subject headings to conduct research, you will be learning by trial and error efficient ways to choose words or combine words. Stay flexible and use your imagination.

CHAPTER 8

Sizing Up Your Sources of Information

(All Sources Are Not Equal)

Before you sit down at a library computer, think through the kinds of sources that are best for your topic, your purpose, and your audience.

■ How to Choose Your Sources

Introductory Versus Specialized Sources

You don't want to read the same basic information in six encyclopedias or six popular magazines. Instead, move on from general reference works to books and periodicals. You may find a book that includes a chapter on your specific topic, or you may find a whole book devoted to your topic.

On the other hand, some sources may be too specialized for you. It is useful to know that the term *magazine* is used for periodicals written for the public (such as *Newsweek* and *Harper's*), whereas the term *journal* is used for periodicals written for and by specialists in the field (such as the *Journal of Popular Culture* and *American Literature*). Although you may be more comfortable reading magazines, your best sources of information may be in the journals appropriate to your topic.

In choosing the level of your sources, consider also your reader's level of expertise. Are you writing for a specialist in the field? If so, you will want to move beyond general information into scholarly journals. But if you are writing for the general public or for a teacher not trained in your specific subject, you should rely more heavily on general or introductory sources.

Books Versus Periodicals

Your subject will determine how much you can rely on books as opposed to periodicals. In general, current periodicals—newspapers, magazines, and journals—are more up-to-date (books take longer to write and to publish); on the other hand, books may provide a better overview and more depth of the subject. Therefore, it's important to use a balance of both books and periodicals in researching most subjects.

Recent Versus Old Sources

Recent sources build on the sources of the past, so it is usually best to work from recent dates backward through the periodical indexes and to begin studying the books with the latest copyright dates. Be aware of whether your source is out-of-date. Do not use a source from 1992 for a paper on current developments in computer design; do not quote someone saying "today" without making clear if the writer's today was fifty years ago. On the Internet, a source from even two days ago may be out of date.

However, there are two major exceptions to this rule:

- **Historical topics.** If you are researching from a historical perspective, you will want to use sources current at that time. You may also want to use retrospective studies, so check periodicals dated around the fifth, tenth, fiftieth, or hundredth anniversaries.

- **Classics in the field.** These are often the first studies or landmark studies in a field. You can find these classics through careful reading; they or their authors will be referred to frequently in later studies.

Primary Versus Secondary Sources

- **Primary sources** are those written by the people actually involved in the subject you are studying. In a study of pioneer women, their diaries and letters are primary sources; so are county records of births, deaths, marriages, and the like. In a study of Martin Luther King, Jr., his speeches and other writings are primary sources.

- **Secondary sources** are those written by people who, like you, were studying the subject. These writers relied as much as possible on primary sources; but they also made an extensive search for important secondary sources about the subject. Secondary sources would include a history of pioneer women or a biography of Martin Luther King, Jr.

In many research projects, you will rely mainly on secondary sources. They are especially useful for providing the context surrounding primary sources. Whenever possible, however, make it a point to read primary source material first and draw your own conclusions before you accept a secondary source's opinion. Also, if a primary source is important to your subject—as in a study of one of Martin Luther King's speeches—it must occupy a prominent position in your paper. Secondary sources can only supplement your careful examination of the primary text.

◾ How to Assess What You've Found

Not all information you come across is fair and accurate. In fact, many writers, businesses, and organizations conduct research and disseminate information that will support their philosophy, point of view, or economic position. Therefore, you should stay alert and look closely for biases in what you are reading. For help in assessing sources of information, see FAIR (Fairness and Accuracy in Reporting) listed in the Appendix of this book.

Books

Before you start reading a book, you need to evaluate what it has and does not have for you. Several parts of the book can tell you quickly if it will meet your needs.

- Check its date by looking at the back of the title page; depending on your topic, you may need more up-to-date information.
- Read the table of contents. Does the book have chapters that relate directly to your angle?
- Look in the index under headings of special concern to you; study the subheadings.

- Read the jacket material and author's biography (back cover or back pages). You can immediately find out who the author is and from what perspective he or she has written the book.

- Look at the preface or introduction. See how the author presents the purpose of the book. The preface may point you to other important books; the introduction may give you an overview of the topic.

- Look specifically for a *bibliography* or *recommended reading* list at the back of the book before the index. Many books supply a list of sources (especially if there are footnotes or endnotes) or other valuable books related to the same subject.

Articles

Your evaluation of an article begins with how you found it. Specialized indexes in the library will find articles that are more scholarly or technical. General indexes (such as those on *InfoTrak*) list articles for the average reader.

- Identify the intended audience. Is the periodical aimed at the general reader or at professionals in the field?

- Is the publication nationally known? If your subject is offbeat, articles from underground newsletters are appropriate; if not, back up the shadow publications with other sources. For academic topics, use scholarly journals.

- How long is the article? Sometimes a few facts are all you need, but in-depth analysis requires length.

- What is the style of the article? Is it dense with technical jargon? Even if you understand it, you may need to translate for your reader. Is it breezy and filled with slang? It may be too lightweight for your report.

- Is the article directly related to your topic or only slightly related? Does it focus on personalities or facts? For example, an article on the restaurant Einstein frequented in Princeton won't help you write a paper on his theories.

The Internet

Information on the Internet can be uneven. If you encounter an author or title repeatedly as you read scholarly publications, you can be fairly certain that these items are highly respected in that field. However, if you encounter repeated authors and titles while searching on the Internet, you can't be certain that these items are necessarily respected by experts in the field; often, Web sites will indicate what is popular or hot information—not necessarily the most reliable.

Your first indication of the quality of an article on the Internet is its address. Look for reputable institutions and for articles that identify the author.

- Addresses ending in *.com* indicate a business. Businesses usually have a bias toward their product or their advertisers. Even prominent newspapers are big businesses, and thus many of their reports can reflect their business bias.

- Addresses ending in *.gov* refer to a government agency. Look at the heading to be sure that the report is authorized.

- Addresses ending in *.edu* (educational institution) are often those of faculty. Check for the identification of the author and the institution. Sometimes students (individually or as a class project) present information that can be quite good and interesting. However, be sure to know if you are reading information put together by students like yourself or if you are reading a professor's lecture notes or a scholarly paper.

- Discussion groups often present valuable information, but you need to verify where the group originated or is located. Is the group devoted to serious discussion? Is the author identified? Does the person give sources? If so, follow some of these leads and assess if the sources are really useful.

Overall, when you are gathering information on the Internet, make it standard practice to know exactly where this information is coming from. Only then will you be in a strong enough position to assess its value for your research.

CHAPTER 9

TAKING NOTES

(THE BRIDGE BETWEEN YOUR SOURCES AND YOUR PAPER)

The key to a readable research paper is creating a blend of your own ideas with those of others. The last thing you want to do is construct your paper with big blocks of information from your sources. Keeping a strong sense of your own ideas and what you are looking for to support these ideas will eliminate hours of scribbling excessive notes that you don't even need. *Good notes*—efficient notes you can ultimately use—are an important bridge between your research and the writing of your final paper.

Don't confuse note-taking with writing a paper. You cannot write your paper as you read your sources without committing plagiarism and creating a disaster. First take your notes; then write your paper. Following this sequence will help you avoid the pitfall of copying or rewording blocks of material and presenting them as your paper.

■ HOW TO TAKE GOOD NOTES

Be Selective

Even though a source is on your topic, it may not have any new or relevant information:

- Don't write down what you already know.
- Don't write down the same general (background) information more than once.
- Don't write down a story or piece of information that is entertaining but that will be useless to your report.

Take Notes Almost Entirely in Your Own Words

Do not copy out whole paragraphs from your sources. You can waste valuable time and energy by laboriously copying out material you never even use—not to mention the wasted time of rereading everything and trying to decide what to use.

Put nearly everything you read into your own words by using *summary* and *paraphrase* (see Chapters 26 and 27). Reserve quotation marks (*direct quotations*) for memorable statements of opinion (see Chapter 25). Reflect on what you read, and then put it into your own words so that it makes sense to you. As you do so, you will be taking the first step toward refining your own ideas and eventually writing your paper.

Use Direct Quotation

Direct quotations are not just something spoken by another person; they are also any words written by another person. Be absolutely vigilant in putting quotation marks around every word that you take from your sources, even if it's only one or two words or half a sentence. If the writer quotes someone else, be sure to note who is being quoted and the source of the quotation.

Get Your Facts Straight

Any statistics and facts must be recorded accurately. Take special care to copy all numbers, names, and other facts correctly, and then check them against the original one more time. Be sure to also record your source of information.

Keep Each Note Brief but Understandable

When you can, write in phrases or short sentences that you will be able to skim quickly. Be sure that each note will make sense to you when you read it later out of the context of the whole article or essay.

Keep an Accurate Record of Documentation

In your final paper, you will need to tell exactly where you found your information; so, as you take notes, write down author, title, and other bibliographical information for every source. (See page 54.) Beside each note, record the exact page number on which you found the information. If the note covers material that runs more than one page, indicate for yourself where the page changes. This habit will ensure that your documentation is fully accurate.

In addition, be clear about the difference between *quotation* (writing down another's exact wording that you enclose in quotation marks) and *documentation* (giving credit for all information whether quoted or not).

◼ USING TECHNOLOGY TO TAKE NOTES

Photocopies

Sometimes a page filled with information is best photocopied, especially if it has an important chart, an extended quotation, or a list of other sources. The advantage of this method is that you can be absolutely sure that you have accurate statistics or direct quotations. The disadvantage is that photocopied material is not in your own words. Therefore, you will need to incorporate it into your own style as you write your paper.

Before you return the source from which you photocopied, be sure to write onto the photocopy all bibliographical data. Also make sure that page numbers are legible.

Taking Notes on Computers

You can transfer material from your sources directly onto the computer. Be sure to note the names of the databases or the Internet addresses and the date you viewed them. (Some programs list this information for you, but be sure to check before you exit.) In some cases you may later be able to transfer quotations and documentation directly into your paper. This method can save you time.

However, the big danger exists that you might construct your paper out of blocks of information lifted from your sources instead of writing a paper that presents your own ideas. Be certain that you record complete bibliographical data and the page number of all notes you type in yourself. Also, keep your own thoughts in a separate section or use a different typeface or a special tag (such as "my idea") to avoid accidental plagiarism.

☐ Flashes of Inspiration

- Take time frequently during your note-taking to stop and write down your own ideas and reactions. Remember that your final paper will be largely your thoughts, not just chunks of information from your sources. You will supply the emphasis, the order of points, the introduction, the evaluation of sources, and the conclusions.

- If you wait until you've done all your reading before you write down your own ideas, you may find that your ideas have flown away. Therefore, seize all good ideas that come to you while you're reading sources or even while you're on the way home from the library. Stop and write them down immediately.

- Do not shortchange your ideas when they come. Write them out in sentences and paragraphs, and you will find that when you sit down to write your paper, some of it is already in a good first draft.

CHAPTER 10

RESEARCHING ON COMPUTERS

(THE BASICS)

The research paper is one assignment for which computer skills are essential. If you're new to using computers for research or you're familiar with only one system, read this chapter before you begin your research. Skip or skim any section that you already understand. If you've never used computers to any extent, you will need to get instruction from your college computer center.

■ GETTING AROUND WITHIN DIFFERENT PROGRAMS

Even if you've used a computer for word processing, you may encounter computer systems where your actions will not bring about the expected results.

Using the Computer Keyboard Only

Some systems respond only to commands that are typed in, using no mouse. You will need to pay attention to the directions on each screen, because programs ask you to use different keys at different times. Sometimes you will

- Type in the number of the item you want.

- Type the highlighted letter of the item.

- Type the word or phrase; press Enter/Return.

- Using an arrow or tab key, highlight the item; press Enter/Return.

Usually, the directions will appear at the bottom of the screen, but sometimes you'll be prompted by a blinking cursor right on the line where you should type. If nothing happens after you have typed something, press Enter/Return.

Using a Mouse

With a mouse-based program (Windows and MacIntosh systems), you mouse-click on highlighted phrases in the text or on *icons* (little symbolic pictures). You will then either press a key, or mouse-click, or type in what you want.

Move the mouse around on the pad until the cursor (arrow or vertical bar) on the screen is positioned on the icon or phrase you want to select; then click once. You will see your selection highlighted on the screen. Click a second time to select the item. When you have to type in a line, position the cursor on the left margin of the space where the first letter should go, and then click the mouse before you type.

▣ Basic Maneuvers with Either Keyboard or Mouse

Selecting

Often you will tell the computer what you want by choosing from a menu (list) of options or by selecting an underlined phrase presented in a different color from the rest of the text. You reach your selection either by moving the mouse or using the arrow keys. You communicate your selection by clicking the mouse or by pressing Enter/Return after the choice is highlighted. With many computer programs, the cursor changes from an arrow to a hand pointing upward to indicate that you can select at that point.

Drop-down Menus

A drop-down menu is a list of choices that appears underneath a particular heading when you click on that heading, such as *Options* or *Commands*. Often, the words appear at the top of your screen. If there is a mouse, highlight (mouse-click) on the heading; then, while holding the mouse button down, drag down to highlight your choice; release the mouse. If there is not a mouse, use Enter/Return and then the arrow keys to select what you want.

Windows

As you are working within a program, you will notice various borders that outline "*windows*" on the screen. You open and close these windows as you move through the program. If there are two or more borders, the one on the inner frame controls the window you're working in. To close a window, click on the X or square in the upper-right corner on a PC or upper-left on a Mac.

Scrolling

To scroll (move vertically through the text) you can use the arrow keys, the Page Up or Page Down keys, or the mouse. To use the mouse, look at the right margin of the innermost window frame. Either position the cursor and click continuously on the arrow pointing in the direction you want to move the text (up or down), or click on the "button" to slide it down the margin as you read. Just click and hold the mouse as you guide it smoothly and in a straight line (towards you to go down; away from you to go up). This method is particularly useful if you want to skim a document quickly. That "button" in the right margin is also a clue to the length of the material you are reading; it will slide down to the bottom margin as you approach the end of the document.

Saving

When you find important information, you can save it onto a disk and then print it out later. It's always better to save material to the computer in small bits rather than in long documents. You will also want to save material to the disk frequently to avoid losing it should there be a problem with the computer.

If you have a sizable research project, you will want to save as much information as possible onto your disk, to avoid needless typing. When you go to the library or computer lab, take a 3.5-inch disk formatted for the system used there (if you know whether it is Mac or PC). Then save each portion of your research as a *document*, and give it an appropriate title so that you can easily find it later.

• Insert your formatted disk into the computer.

• Click on Save or Record at the top of the screen; it may be under Options or Commands.

• Name each file with a different name, and write down the full title and Internet address (because you can't enter any of your own writing directly on this file yet).

• If you are working in a library or computer lab, be sure to save your notes in *text-only* format, both to save space and to make sure that your word-processing program can read them.

• Some libraries or computer labs may not allow you to use your own disk; if not, try to print the files you want.

• **Be extra careful to avoid plagiarism when you are saving materials on computers.** Put each source into a separate document, and add complete and accurate information so that you can acknowledge it in your final paper.

Error Messages

Many programs alert you with a sound effect if you're trying to perform something that won't work. Others will give an error message. Click on Help (or type Ctrl +h or Ctrl + ?) to learn what to do.

Exit

When you enter a program, note the command (frequently Alt + F4) that tells you how to exit or quit. If you forget, you can usually try Ctrl + Q or mouse-click on the X or square in the top-right or top-left corner. Don't just turn off your computer, particularly if you're connected to a text-based host computer program. It can leave the line busy for others.

CHAPTER 11

How to Conduct a Computer Search

(Using Search Strings)

It's exciting and easy to search for information using computers, often to the point that it doesn't feel like work at all. However, it can also be frustrating and time-consuming if you don't know what to expect.

There are two common methods of searching: moving from menu to menu and writing search strings. Menus are easier to use, but search strings are often more productive.

■ Searching Through Menus

Often during electronic searches you will see a list of topics; click on one and you will see a list of subtopics; click on one and you'll see sub-subtopics, and so forth. This method is good for a start, but it is not as precise as combining search terms.

■ Typing in Your Subject

In most library catalogs, databases, and Internet search engines, you will see a horizontal box outline on the screen; this is where you type the phrases you want the computer programs to hunt for. Every search program uses slightly different rules of operation, but most use *Boolean operators* such as *and* and *or* to tell the computer how to interpret your list of search terms. Check the directions or helpline of the program before beginning. Some programs will allow you to use a long string of phrases, linked by punctuation; others may have a limit.

In general:

- **Don't use capitals.**

- **Truncate endings** (omit *-s, -ed, -ing, -able, -ial, -y/ies* endings). Sometimes you'll give the root word and an asterisk to indicate variations (*mercur**).

- **Use *and* to connect two terms that must both appear** (*mercury and fish*). If you are told that "Boolean *and* is implied," then just put a space between all the words you want (toxic mercury fish).

- **Use *or* to link two terms,** either of which must appear (*fish or seafood*).

- **Use *not* to exclude any terms you don't want** (*mercury* not *car* not *planet*).

- **Omit other connectors,** such as *with, of,* or *between.*

- **Use punctuation**—quotation marks, parentheses, or brackets—to join words into a phrase. When you use quotation marks to enclose a phrase, the terms marked this way would have to occur together, in the order specified:

    (*underwater archaeology*)   {*fried green tomatoes*}
    "*chrysler building*"

- **Some searchers allow you to specify a date:**

    1985–1996 - means 1985 *through* 1996

    1985, 1996 - means 1985 *and* 1996

- **Some search programs use symbols instead of connecting words:**

    and (+ or &)   *not* (- or !)   *or* (|)   *near* (^)

These symbols are all capitals of the numerals on the top row of the keyboard; place the symbol immediately before the word you are designating, without spaces. However, check the helpline to find out which symbols to use.

For example, if you entered the following as your search

mercur* or "mercury poisoning"

and

fish or seafood not car not automobile not planet

or alternatively

mercur*|(mercury poisoning)+fish|seafood-car-automobile-planet

it would mean that you want those documents discussing any words with the *mercur-* base—such as *mercury, mercuric, mercurial*—or the phrase *"mercury poisoning"* plus the words *fish* or *seafood*, but—to eliminate references to Mercury—not any about cars or planets.

Using your search string, phrase your search. Beginning with the more specific phrase, list the words you want the computer to search for, according to the guidelines on the program you're using. Keep rephrasing your search until you get a manageable (fifty or less) list of sources.

You will usually need to do several searches with different keywords, narrowing down your search so that you get more and more specific information.

■ WHAT IF THERE IS NO MATCH FOR YOUR REQUEST?

- **Check your spelling.** You may have misspelled one or more words.

- **Check your symbols and phrasing.** You may have used the wrong symbols or phrasing for that particular search engine. Check the directions or helpline.

- **Use more general terms.** You may have submitted too narrow a search. Try generalizing a bit—for example, change the phrase *"mercury level in tuna"* to *mercury and tuna,* or add alternatives (*seafood or fish*).

- **Use both the abbreviation and the full name.** Give the abbreviation and the full name, linked by *or* (*CIA or "Central Intelligence Agency"*).

- **Check your search engine or database.** You may have selected an inappropriate search engine or database. See the Appendix of this book for some suggestions, according to topic.

- **Information is there but you can't access it during the session.** The information may be at a location that is either down or experiencing heavy usage. Your computer server may be experiencing a slowdown, again due to heavy usage. Try again later.

◼ WHAT IF YOU GET TOO MANY LISTINGS?

- **Take a look at the first ten to see if they coincide at all with your topic.** For instance, if your inquiry on mercury yielded dozens of articles, and the first ten are all about the planet Mercury, you'll need to rephrase the search string or use a different listing.

- **Add more words to your search string.**

    toxicologist and *marine* and *FDA* and *mercury* and *seafood*

    When possible, link (+) the terms so that all will appear in your selected documents.

- **Specify terms that you do not want.**

    mercury   not automobile   not planet

- **Replace common words with technical terms or phrases specific to your topic.**

    Hg or mercury   ppm   "methyl mercury"   "predatory fish"

- **Use the search engine's "Advanced Search" or "Refine Search" options; check for specific instructions.**

See the Appendix in this book for a listing of databases and search engines.

☐ WHAT COMPUTERS CAN AND CANNOT DO

Research programs are user-friendly, so you'll often get plenty of information quickly. However, you still need to be creative in how you tell the computer what to look for.

Computers Can	What You Must Do
Scan a vast number of documents rapidly.	Determine the best words to use for scanning documents.
Narrow your search.	Articulate the limits of your search.
Allow you to download files in your report.	Save the files on your disk; record bibliographic information.

Computers Cannot	What You Must Do
Find something that is listed under a different term.	Use synonyms; suggest more general topics; be creative in phrasing your search.
Find something that isn't there.	Recognize that some material isn't available electronically; carefully select the databases you search.
Correct a misspelled word.	Type carefully and proofread zealously; use alternate spelling when appropriate.
Discriminate between different meanings, such as *Mercury* (the car or planet) and *mercury* (the mineral).	Add words preceded by *not* so you can eliminate unwanted usage of your search terms.
Provide context.	Add terms and punctuation that provide context, such as *"toxic mercury."*

CHAPTER 12

In a Crunch 2
(Last-Minute Search Strategies)

☐ Be Realistic at the Start about the Time You Have

Time is short, so don't take on something you're clearly not going to have the time to do. For example, you can't sit down and read a 400-page book on your topic if you have only a week left in which to write the whole paper.

☐ If You're New to Computers

Limit your use of them to the library catalog. Use listings in bound volumes rather than trying to search online.

☐ If You Find No Sources Listed

Try different synonyms—different terms for your subject.

☐ If You Find Too Many Sources

Try subtopics that appear under your subject heading. Also, narrow down your topic even further by limiting it to time and place—for example, Major Oil Spills in Louisiana from 1980–1990.

☐ Use a Mix of Sources

Look for a mix of books and articles, introductory and advanced material; for last-minute research, stick with recent information. Gather a couple of extra sources (beyond the minimum required) in case a source turns out to be useless.

☐ TAKE NOTES ON A COMPUTER AND USE PHOTOCOPIES

You don't have a lot of spare time for handwriting long notes. Bring your own *formatted* disk to the computer lab and take notes from your sources right in the library. Also photocopy source material rather than taking notes. But be certain to record all bibliographic information. Remember that downloaded and photocopied material cannot be put directly into your paper without risking plagiarism and creating an unreadable paper.

☐ MAKE FRIENDS WITH A LIBRARIAN

Your most direct route to usable information is a sympathetic librarian. He or she can help you enormously by taking you straight to materials that relate to your topic. You'll save yourself hours of wandering around in a maze.

PART 3

EXPLORING DIFFERENT AVENUES OF RESEARCH

CHAPTER 13

SLEUTHING FOR VALUABLE RESOURCES

(START YOUR SEARCH OUTSIDE THE LIBRARY)

Many of us enjoy watching or reading detective stories and trying to figure out clues, yet we rarely get the challenge of doing our own detective work. Research is detection, requiring a detective's persistence and flashes of insight. Sleuthing means that you will check all the usual sources—in this case, books and reference works—and it also means that you will track down some surprising sources. One source leads you to other sources; one seemingly insignificant fact leads you to whole areas of investigation.

Although the library is the place where you'll find the most information under one roof, many valuable sources of information are available to you both in and near your home.

☐ NETWORKING

Networking requires only that you let others in on what you want to know. Tell your classmates, your friends, and all your relatives about your project and enlist their help in alerting you to source material, people you could interview, or places where you might look.

☐ THE TELEPHONE BOOK

You can locate businesses and organizations that you can call or visit to get free brochures and other information. Suppose you're starting your research on a broad topic such as cruelty to animals. You can look in the yellow pages, get the phone numbers and addresses of local animal-rights organizations, and then call and visit them. Most organizations will give you free brochures and reprints of articles, surveys, and so forth, which, in turn, will aid you in getting a more specific focus for your topic.

You can also locate specific people who will grant you an interview, either over the telephone or in person—doctors, psychologists, heads of day-care centers, directors of laboratories, and so forth.

☐ Toll-Free Telephone Numbers

Check the list of directories in the Appendix of this book or call 1-800-555-1212 for the toll-free telephone numbers of specific associations or companies that might offer brochures or information services related to your topic. Often you are able to get information over the phone and can list that source as an interview on your Works Cited page.

☐ Query Letters or E-Mail Messages

You can write brief letters or e-mail messages requesting information from specific organizations or individuals. However, you must allow at least a week to get a reply. Be certain to keep your query brief, never more than two paragraphs. List the information you request item by item for ease in replying; limit your request to the essentials. If you use regular mail, enclose a self-addressed, stamped envelope with your letter, and keep a copy of the letter for your records.

☐ On-Site Visits

Make appointments with local businesses or institutions for on-site visits. For example, if you're researching day-care centers, visit a day-care center and observe how it is run. Don't be shy about asking. Most people are happy to take a break in their day and give information to others.

☐ Specialized Museums, Libraries, Historical Societies, and Organizational Headquarters

Nonprofit organizations often have libraries open to the public. For example, in New York City, the American Kennel Club Library has materials on all registered breeds of dogs. The Old Court House Museum in Vicksburg, Mississippi, has an important collection of Civil War artifacts. The North Plains Historical Society Museum in Canyon, Texas, has Native American and pioneer artifacts.

☐ SPECIALIZED NEWSLETTERS

There are newsletters for every subject imaginable. The best way to find newsletters on your topic is via the Internet, but you can also phone associations or businesses and ask if they have a newsletter they will share with you. The public relations or customer services office can usually tell you what newsletters are available.

☐ GOVERNMENT PUBLICATIONS

As an American citizen, you have the right to a wide variety of information. Here are a few ways to learn what is available:

- **Call the Federal Information telephone number: 1-800-688-9889.** Or check http://www.fedworld.gov

- **Call your congressional office.** Your congressional representative maintains a staff, part of whose job is to provide information for constituents. These staff members know how to locate government studies, reports of commissions, and statistics. They can help with topics of national or local interest.

- **Call other government offices.** Your state representative, your mayor's office, your county extension agent, and specific departments (Board of Education, Department of Consumer Affairs, Environmental Protection Agency, State Attorney General's office, Bureau of Vital Statistics, and so forth) have information that is available to you. You can get a monthly catalog of publications on all sorts of topics, from farming to home construction, from the United States Government Printing Office in Washington, DC, 20401 (202-512-0000) or from your library's reference section.

- **Visit your county courthouse.** In the courthouse you can find the proceedings of court cases that deal with issues you may be investigating. In addition, you have the right to examine wills, deeds, and other public documents that provide valuable facts about people and places you may be studying.

☐ Public Radio and Television

Public radio and television provide an amazing array of information on a variety of topics. You can get transcripts by mail for a small fee or sometimes free from Web sites. See the Appendix of this book or call your local station.

☐ Videotapes, Photographs, and Illustrations

You can now get a videotape on nearly any topic. Similarly, still photographs, illustrations, and even cartoons may illuminate your topic. Some of this material can be photocopied and inserted into your paper; other material might be better described. For example, the film *The Pawnbroker* reveals how Spanish Harlem looked in 1967; Walker Evans's photographs show how many rural families lived in the South during the Depression.

☐ Lectures and Talks

Another good source that you might overlook is notes you've taken during class lectures or while attending a presentation. Be certain, however, that your notes are accurate and that any quotation you attribute to the speaker is exact.

☐ Unusual Sources

Don't ignore popular reference books such as the *Guinness Book of World Records* and the *Farmer's Almanac*. For example, information on the oldest living human being could provide useful facts in a paper on aging, health, nutrition, or smoking.

Check the Appendix in this book for a selected list of unusual sources.

CHAPTER 14

THE LIBRARY 1
(GETTING STARTED)

Even if you're under a deadline, don't just rush pell-mell into the library and frantically grab anything you can find. The great danger in a trip to the library is that if you don't know what you are looking for, you can get lost in a maze of catalogs, databases, books, and articles.

■ FOCUS YOUR SEARCH BEFORE YOU BEGIN

Before you head for the library, make sure you have done the preliminary writing that will focus your search:

- Freewrite to discover your angle on the topic.

- Write down the questions you want to answer in your research.

- Make a list of subject headings you can use for computer searches.

These preliminary steps—the work of a few hours at most—will save you from wandering around the library, following irrelevant leads, and changing your topic half a dozen times. Instead, you will enter the library with a clear idea of what you want to find out.

■ USE A GENERAL REFERENCE TO GET AN OVERVIEW

For many topics, a good place to start is the reference section of the library. Although your teacher may prohibit citing encyclopedias or dictionaries in the final version of your paper, reading an article in a general reference book will give you a quick overview of your topic.

As you read, jot down key words that you might later look up as subtopics. Look also for specific suggested readings. Finally, consider your list of questions; the reference book may lead you to new, more precise questions to add to the list.

Here are some reference works to consider:

- **Encyclopedias and dictionaries.** For a general encyclopedia, *Encyclopaedia Britannica* is most often cited; it is available in bound volumes and on computers in your library. For a general dictionary, *Webster's Unabridged* is most often cited. The library also has many specialized encyclopedias and dictionaries; you will find some of these listed in the library catalog.

- **Biographical materials.** Start with *Who's Who*, which comes in a number of volumes corresponding to countries and professions, or with a biographical dictionary such as the *Dictionary of American Biography*. The *Biography and General Master Index* lists biographical articles located in a wide variety of sources.

- **Specialized reference books.** Just about every field has specialized reference books; consult the Appendix of this book, the reference librarian, or a teacher.

■ KEEP A WORKING BIBLIOGRAPHY

The moment you even touch a book or magazine or read information online, stop and write down (preferably on a 3×5 card so that you can easily alphabetize them) *all* bibliographical information:

- **Author** (last name first)

- **Title of book or article** (for article, also record title of periodical)

- **Publishing information** (city, publisher, year of publication for book; complete date for periodical)

- **Page numbers** (for articles or chapters; plus section number for newspapers and volume number for scholarly journals)

Even if you think you won't use a particular source in your paper, write it down anyway. You may find it useful after all—at least as a contrasting example.

■ OTHER LIBRARY SERVICES

Book Request

If you cannot find a book in the stacks, ask at the circulation desk to see if the book is checked out or misplaced. If it is checked out, leave your name, and the library will hold the book for you when it's returned.

Books on Reserve

Sometimes a teacher requests that materials for a specific class be kept on reserve. These materials are available for a shorter borrowing time than usual—two hours, for instance, or overnight. Often they are kept in a separate reserve room.

Interlibrary Loan

If you identify a book or article that your library does not have, ask at the circulation desk for the person who handles interlibrary loans. The librarian can get the materials for you, often within days.

Computer Lab

Besides the computerized catalog, periodical indexes, and other databases, most libraries have a section where you can use computers to write papers, log onto the Internet, and consult CD-ROMs.

Pamphlets and Clippings

The pamphlet file (*vertical* or *clippings* file) is an accumulation of pamphlets, articles, and brochures. It is an especially good source of material pertaining to local areas such as your state or home town. For help with locating materials in the vertical file, consult the *Vertical File Index*, a monthly publication that lists maps, posters, and articles under both subject and title.

Films and Other Audiovisual Materials

Films, computer programs, recordings, tapes, and filmstrips are usually located in a separate section of the library. You can also find these materials through the library catalog.

Services to Accommodate Disabilities

If you have need for materials in a special format (large print or audiotapes of print materials, closed-captioned videos, or adapted computers for physical limitations), the library has them or can help you request them. The *New York Times* has a limited edition each week in large print. Other computer programs will vocalize the words for you. Volunteer organizations will tape printed materials for you or type your dictated material if you provide enough lead time. Check with the librarian.

CHAPTER 15

THE LIBRARY 2
(TRACKING DOWN BOOKS AND ARTICLES)

Hometown libraries are useful for having the best-known books and references and for local history and other topics of local concern. However, college libraries are preferable for research into most academic topics since they usually have larger collections and specialized periodicals.

☐ HOW TO FIND BOOKS

Use the Library Catalogs

Books, media holdings, and reference materials are cataloged by *author, title,* and *subject.* At least in the beginning, you probably will be using the subject catalog to locate books and authors. On the computer, you can find a list of books relating to your subject. Follow the system's instructions to see a *brief display,* listing several books, or to see a *full display,* giving detailed information about each book. Once you have the display you want, use the printer (if available) to get a listing for each entry. This way you're certain to have an accurate record of each book for later use and the call number that you'll use to help you locate the book. Otherwise, you'll need to write down the author, title, and call number.

Become Familiar with Library Classification Systems

- **Library of Congress** Most colleges and universities use the Library of Congress classification system. In this system the call number begins with two letters of the alphabet. For example, *Pocahontas's Daughters: Gender and Ethnicity in American C͏͏* Mary V. Dearborn has the call number, PS 147 D ′ 3

- **Dewey Decimal System** Most public libraries use the Dewey Decimal System. Call numbers in this system begin with numbers rather than with letters. For example, *Pocahontas's Daughters* has the call number, 810.99 2.D.

Allow Time for Browsing

Once you have the call numbers for the books you want, you're ready to head to the stacks, the main area of the library where books are housed. Take a few minutes to browse through the books on the shelf. Sometimes you will find a valuable book on the same shelf as others that you found through the catalog. Check the backs of a number of books for *bibliographies,* listings of other books and articles in the field.

Too Many or Too Few Books

- **When you can't find any book on your subject.** Don't give up. Look under all possible related subject headings. Check the reference section of the library for more general sources. If all else fails, *ask the librarian for help*—always your most important emergency tactic.

- **When the book is not on the shelf.** Ask the circulation desk to reserve the book for you when it is returned, or see if it is available through interlibrary loan.

- **When you find too many books.** Reconsider your subject heading. Can you narrow it? You may be able to eliminate many of the books by their titles (either too general or too restrictive) or by their dates. Check the most recent first. Ask a teacher or other experts in the field which are the most valuable books. And, remember, the preface and acknowledgments of recent books may ͨ classics in the field.

☐ HOW TO FIND ARTICLES

Use Periodical Indexes

To find a book, use the catalog; to find an article in a magazine or newspaper, use an *index.*

A special section or room in your library houses many types of indexes. These indexes are kept on computer or in large volumes, usually one volume for each year, with subjects listed alphabetically.

- Computerized listings are faster to use and allow you to combine subject headings. However, they have the disadvantage that they cover articles written only since approximately 1980.

- Print format sometimes is more complete than the computerized equivalent and goes further back in time. You'll also find browsing easier on printed pages.

In either format—computer or print—you will need to try a variety of headings that fit your topic. Under each heading you will find a list of articles on that subject; in abbreviated form, each entry will tell you the title of the article, the title of the periodical, the date of the publication, and the pages on which the article appears.

Here are some indexes with which you should be familiar:

Reader's Guide to Periodical Literature (in bound volumes) and *InfoTrak* (on computer) cover articles from magazines written for the general public, such as *Newsweek, Popular Mechanics,* and *Psychology Today. InfoTrak* also covers major newspapers such as the *New York Times* and *The Wall Street Journal.*

The *New York Times Index,* published since 1851, is an annual index of all subjects covered in the *Times.* This alphabetical list of subjects gives the title, date, section, page, and column for each article. The *index* is useful for recent information, since the *Times* publishes informative articles on science, international affairs, business, and other contemporary subjects. It is also useful for historical topics, guiding you to complete texts of major speeches, reports of battles and elections, reviews of performances, stock prices, box scores, and so forth.

Specialized listings cover articles in scholarly journals, written by experts in each field. Articles in these journals are listed by subject in specialized indexes such as *Humanities Index, General Sciences Index,* and *Social Sciences Index.* Each discipline has its own listings. For instance, the *MLA Bibliography* (published annually by the Modern Language Association) lists books and articles about literature.

Citation indexes allow you to find out what experts consider the classics in their field. They indicate which older articles were referred to in other articles each year. Citation indexes are organized by discipline: *Humanities Citation Index, Science Citation Index,* and *Social Sciences Citation Index.*

Full text databases include the whole text, not just the title. Understandably, there are few available for free. See the Appendix of this book for sites to check.

Statistical sources (CD-ROM or print) are a fast way to find statistical information. For example, see the Census Bureau data in the *1990 Census of Population and Housing, The County and City Databook,* or *USA Counties, 1994.*

Directories (CD-ROM or print) include information found in phone books but also sort the information by categories, giving you leads to further research. For example, you can see lists of businesses by type, giving corporate officers and annual sales figures. Check your library for *Dun's Business Locator, Dun's Small Business Sourcing File,* and *Standard and Poor's Corporations.*

The Appendix of this book presents many listings that you can consult.

Locating Articles in the Library

When you have copied down or printed out a list of articles, you'll then ha~~ ~o find them in the library. The computerized indexes will often   ~ther the library carries the periodical and even the lo~   or article. Otherwise, consult the *holdings file,*
~als your library has. Before you copy down
~e journal, make sure that your library
~eed an article from a journal that your
librarian whether the article can be

Magazines, scholarly journals, and newspapers are housed in several ways:

- Current issues are in the periodical reading room, a separate location where you can take the current issue off the shelf and sit down to read it.

- Recent back issues of magazines and newspapers are kept in their original format.

- Back issues going further back in time either are bound into volumes and kept on the shelves in the reference section or are available on microform or CD-ROM.

CHAPTER 16

INTRODUCTION TO THE INTERNET

(THE BASICS)

You already may be familiar with the Internet. If not, this chapter will introduce you to the basic terms and get you started.

■ DEFINITIONS: SOME KEY TERMS

The **Internet** is the network through which all of the computers in the world can communicate with each other.

- Some of the computers on the Internet provide the interconnections for networks of personal computers, such as a university mainframe computer or America Online.

- Other computers on the Internet provide information from businesses, government agencies, or nonprofit organizations.

Connecting to the Internet allows you access to libraries and museums, computer software, elaborate graphics. Further, you can reach thoughtful and generous people who will respond to your questions.

A **modem** is an electronic device in each computer that uses the telephone lines to transmit the data between computers.

Online means that the computer you are using is communicating with another computer, for example, to connect to the Internet or to access   ' regularly updated catalog and other resources. You are   you are using a computer for word processing

steps you follow to get online (by typing in
ugh certain prescribed steps depending
connect), you type certain words or
mbol.

The **World Wide Web (WWW)** is the fastest-growing area of the Internet. This is the name for the interlinked part of the Internet where you can with one keystroke jump from one topic and location to another. As you scroll through the text, you encounter underlined and colored words or phrases; when you click your mouse (or press the Enter/Return key) on that phrase, you jump to a different page relevant to that topic.

For example, you might start looking at the home page (the first page) of the National Register of Historic Places at the U.S. Department of the Interior; then you might jump from there to a list of landmarked buildings; next you could see a picture of a specific building. Later, you might wonder how you got there, but the computer program allows you to go back to each previous screen, where each of the phrases you clicked on (links) will have changed color, so you can almost always retrace your path until you disconnect.

Web sites are locations on the World Wide Web. There are millions of Web sites, each giving information about a specific topic, organization, product, or program. *Home page* refers to the first page of a Web site and also to your own point of entry to the Internet.

E-mail (electronic mail) is the method of sending messages via computer, either to one person or to a group of people, once you know the correct Internet address. Computers make it possible to send copies simultaneously to a great many people, even allowing for "live chats," where individuals type messages back and forth; many others can read those messages, either at the time or later.

Downloading is the term for copying a document from another computer to your disk or the hard drive of your computer. We speak of computers as *loading* data from a disk or another computer. Thus a Web page is loading onto your computer as it gradually comes into view. You can't scroll through or save a document while it is loading. Should you choose to save it, you would then download a copy of that page onto your own disk. Programs usually provide a visual clue to the status of downloading—for example, with a horizontal bar graph, shooting stars (Netscape), or a spinning pyramid (America Online).

Browsing and surfing are the terms for moving from one Web site to another. Special software, a Web browser (such as Microsoft Explorer or Netscape Navigator), makes it possible for you to reach a Web site by typing in its address or clicking on a highlighted phrase in a Web page.

☐ CONNECTING TO THE INTERNET

To use the Internet, you can go to either a library, a college computer lab, or a commercial establishment that has Internet access. To send and receive e-mail, you will need a personal account—free if your college or local library offers it, or from a commercial service through the World Wide Web. Check different search engines for "free e-mail"—either as a button you select or as a query you type in. Internet access is also available for a monthly fee from online services such as American Online or Microsoft Network.

EQUIPMENT NEEDED TO CONNECT TO THE INTERNET

If you want to use the Internet from home, you will need:

- A computer with at least eight megabytes of memory
- A modem plus communications software to use it
- A phone line, or a hard wire connection if your college provides it
- Additional software, which your Internet server usually provides

Optional Equipment Recommended for the World Wide Web

- A color monitor.
- A sound card (already built into Macintosh computers) and multimedia software if you want to use multimedia sources.

INTERNET ACCOUNTS: USER NAME AND PASSWORD

When you open an Internet account, either with your college or with a commercial online service, you will be asked to submit a user name and password so you can log on and receive e-mail. The user name

(ID or user id) plus your server's address will be your e-mail address on the Internet (usually username@server address, such as wienbrd@sunynassau.edu).

Your password is the sequence of letters or numbers, or a combination of letters and numbers, that you type in to gain access to your account. Since you'll be using it often, select one that is easy to remember and quick to type—and one that others won't be likely to guess. Be sure to type both your user name and password carefully during the initial setup, because what you type is the only sequence the computer will recognize ever after, and write both down in a safe location (not in your computer files).

A BRIEF GUIDE TO INTERNET ADDRESSES

The Internet address (sequence of letters and numbers you type to send e-mail or to reach another computer on the Internet) is based on an established system, DNS (Domain Name System). The last three digits designate the type of institution at the Internet address:

.edu is used by educational institutions.

.org is used by non-profit organizations.

.gov is used by governmental agencies.

.mil is used by the military.

.com is used by commercial organizations.

.net is used by large computer networks.

These addresses assume that the site is in the United States. In addition, you may encounter addresses that end in a two-letter country code, such as ca (Canada), uk (Great Britain), de (Germany), or fr (France).

You can figure out some addresses for World Wide Web sites; try a simple name with the appropriate prefix and suffix. For example, you can reach these Web sites by typing their fairly obvious addresses:

Earthwatch	*http://www.earthwatch.org*
FAA	*http://www.faa.gov*
New York Times	*http://www.nytimes.com*

TYPING REMINDERS

Use the exact sequence of letters and punctuation of the Internet address. A mistake can take you to the wrong location or to nowhere at all.

- Check each character before pressing Enter/Return.

- Use no spaces.

- Use no period at the end (there may be a slash/).

- Use lowercase unless told that the program is case sensitive or if you are copying an obvious capital in an Internet address.

- Use the shift key (not the CapsLock key) for the upper symbol on the number or punctuation keys.

- Be careful to distinguish between the letter l and the number **1**, the hyphen (-) and the underline (_), which is above the hyphen.

- The ~ symbol is the Spanish tilde, above the grave accent (`), at the top left of the keyboard.

- Slashes (diacritical marks //) are forward slashes, at the bottom right of the keyboard.

- Within Web sites, you can click on "buttons" on the margins of the page you're looking at:

   Back takes you to the previous page.

   Forward goes to the next page, after you've moved back.

   Reload gets the Web site back on your screen.

   Bookmark (also called *favorites* or *hotlist*) saves the address of the Web site.

   Home gets you to the home page of your server—your college, library, or on-line service.

   History or **Go** lists the sites already visited.

   Stop interrupts downloading or the attempt to reach a site, necessary during a slowdown.

- The **X** or **square** in the top right-hand corner of the screen (or top-left for Mac) allows you to exit quickly.

A WORD ABOUT INTERNET COURTESY

Although the Internet often feels huge and impersonal, your behavior will affect other people. Communication between computers means you're using the time and energy (*bandwidth*) of other computers whenever you log on or connect to a Web site.

Here are a few ground rules based on the democratic spirit of the Internet:

- Don't tax the system by typing in addresses carelessly.

- Don't surf areas you have no real interest in.

- Log off properly so you do not leave lines busy for other users.

- Use a domestic site (whenever available) in preference to a foreign one.

- Download at offpeak times and at the highest speed you can obtain.

- Honor the time limits when using a library computer, especially during peak usage.

- Empty your e-mail regularly; select preferences that limit the flow of junk mail into your box.

- Cancel subscriptions to Listservs and Usenet groups when your interest has waned.

- When visiting a newsgroup, read the FAQs (list of Frequently Asked/Answered Questions) first; then "lurk" for several days to learn acceptable behavior for that group before you join in.

- You may have heard of *flaming*, an abusive or sarcastic response to a posting on the Internet. Some groups accept and even encourage such a tone, but many do not. It's best to avoid such behavior at all times.

CHAPTER 17

SEARCHING THE INTERNET

(USING SEARCH ENGINES AND OTHER AVENUES)

☐ SEARCH ENGINES

Searches on the World Wide Web are conducted by powerful computer programs called *search engines.*

No matter what program connects you to the Internet, you will probably be given a series of choices for searching the Internet. You can usually press Enter/Return or mouseclick on "search" at the top of your screen, but you may also be given a list of search engines to select from, such as Webcrawler, Excite, Yahoo, Magellan, or AltaVista. Click on the search engine's name, or use the list of metasearchers in the Appendix in this book.

Try several different search engines, because the same search terms will yield different results. You might find enough information to digest right away. If you do, skim the articles quickly and save the useful ones to your disk. To use a search engine, you can work through the subject menus offered on the screen, or you can type a "string" of search terms that narrows down your subject (see Chapter 11, "How to Conduct a Computer Search").

An Example

A search for

> *mercury and seafood or fish*

yielded more than 48,000 articles with the search engine InfoSeek and more than 38,000 with AltaVista, sorted with the most relevant first (meaning the ones the computer program matched best to the query terms). Don't be put off by those numbers; sometimes it's fastest to read a few of the topmost articles, then narrow the search. For example, one of the top articles discussed a study of Finnish men with mercury poisoning. Adding "Scandinavia or Finn" to the search string brought up new articles and then more new search terms.

▣ OTHER AVENUES ON THE INTERNET

RESEARCH SERVICES

There are a number of research services that provide free searches and then charge for copies of the articles. Most of these sites require you to register (give your name and other information) but do not require an initial fee. After you complete your search, you can then go to your library for the article. A good one to try is CARL (Colorado Alliance of Research Libraries; at http://www.carl.org).

HOME PAGES OF COLLEGES AND UNIVERSITIES

More and more college faculty members use the Internet as part of their courses. Try searching with terms from the academic course appropriate to your topic. You may find a syllabus or reading list that will help you in your research.

WEB SITES OF GOVERNMENTAL AND OTHER NONPROFIT ORGANIZATIONS

Some governmental and nonprofit organizations—such as The Smithsonian Institute, The Library of Congress, and National Public Radio—offer information about a wide variety of subjects. Check the Appendix in this book or the Internet Yellow Pages to find Web sites of organizations devoted to your subject area. Often the links will lead you to alternate sources of information.

GOPHERS

This is an easy way to find sites on the Internet. Gopher is a menu system—meaning that you have a list of choices to select, connecting you each time to research facilities appropriate to your subject. A good place to start is with the University of Minnesota, where gophers began: type gopher://gopher.tc.umn.edu to get a list of libraries. Type in the general subject and get a list of related sites. You then click on the one you want and go directly to it.

A gopher often gets results faster than the search engines because it bypasses complex graphics, but that also means it will miss many sites on the Web.

TELNET

Telnet is an older method of communicating on the Internet. Even though Telnet can be difficult to use, some very good libraries and usergroups are available only through Telnet. If your library or computer lab does not provide detailed written instructions, ask a librarian or technical staff member for help.

You will need the Telnet address. You usually encounter one on a Web site, but check http://www.einet.net for a directory.

E-MAIL

Newsgroups (Usenet)

People communicate regularly on the Internet, and some are highly knowledgeable about the subject being discussed. One way to get in on the conversation is to read the postings on a BBS (bulletin board server) or newsgroup (a forum devoted to a particular topic, on which people send in their comments by e-mail). However, for research purposes, you need to be cautious. Anyone can claim to be an authority; so be prepared to check a second source to back up what you get from a newsgroup.

Deja News

The fastest way to get information from newsgroups is to use Deja News Research Service (http://www.dejanews.com), which allows you to search for a specific topic (thread) previously discussed in all newsgroups or those you specify. This way you don't have to wait for e-mail, and you don't have to search the archives of the individual newsgroups. You can ask a very specific question on Deja

News—such as, "Why are barns painted red?"—and get a variety of answers, including the right one. The service also gives good advice on how to conduct the search.

Live Chats

The online services organize a number of *chat rooms* for their members. You may not always get reliable information from chat room discussions, but you will usually get a number of leads.

Query by E-Mail

You can send a direct question to a known expert in the area of your research. To discover Internet addresses for the names of people you encountered in your research, consult one of the Internet directories (see the Appendix). Many individuals don't answer cold-call queries, but a respectful and intelligent question might yield a response.

How to Attract Replies to Your Questions

First check FAQs or Archives. You may get answers to your questions to a newsgroup by reviewing the FAQs (Frequently Asked Questions) or the archives (previous messages or postings sent), available through Deja News or listed when you subscribe.

Observe the level of discussion. Be sure to read previous messages or to follow the ongoing discussion for a few days before sending an e-mail query yourself. You'll invite negative responses if you ask a question that is redundant or inappropriate. Since some mailing lists are really scholarly conferences by e-mail, check carefully before attempting to participate.

Send substantive messages. A well-phrased subject line assures that the message will be read by people who are interested in that topic. Many people ignore messages with vague or emotional subject lines (such as "I need help!" or "I agree"). Give a concise indication of your message: "Request anecdotes on distance learning."

CAUTIONS

The Internet can take up all of your research time. If you're not careful, you can get lost—adding too many subtopics or switching to new topics until your project loses its shape and you've run out of time. Researching electronically can become a mesmerizing activity, and you might find that at the end of a pleasant afternoon there is nothing to report. Consider setting a timer (some computers have this feature installed), stopping every hour to make sure you have something concrete.

The Internet is not a substitute for reading. Be sure you balance your Internet articles with books and periodicals. Many subjects are absent or treated only superficially on the Internet. Allow time during your research to use the library where you will need to find and read most of your sources—and perhaps get a librarian's help.

There is a lot of junk on the Internet. Although there are many legitimate Web sites from government agencies and well-known sources, the quality and accuracy of statements on the Internet vary widely. No one checks or credits the information in chat rooms and most bulletin boards.

Web sites are not like video games. They don't necessarily progress to higher and higher levels. A good source might lead you to a superficial source. You may follow a promising lead and find notes from a scholarly seminar on your topic or just as easily find someone's family portrait or rambling travelogue.

You may never be able to return to some Web sites. Be methodical about using bookmarks if your system allows them; otherwise write down each Internet address with the title of the article.

Beware of paying fees with a credit card. If you do decide to download for a fee, make sure that your credit-card number will be encrypted (scrambled). If it is not, you will be warned that you are about to submit an insecure document. By law, a telephone number must be given so that you can phone in your order.

Remember your angle on your topic and stick to it. Do not change topics just because you come across a new, related topic on a Web site. Skip material that is only loosely related to your specific research questions.

CHAPTER 18

CONDUCTING INTERVIEWS
(TO GET BEHIND THE SCENES)

At first you might feel intimidated about calling someone who is important and probably too busy to grant an interview. Actually, many people like to be interviewed; if you're persistent and use good sense and good manners, chances are that you can get an interview with almost anybody you set your heart on.

▣ HOW TO GET AN INTERVIEW WITH ALMOST ANYONE

Pinpoint the Person You'd Like to Interview

First decide which person you'd most like to interview. Then write down exactly what you'd like to find out from him or her. The information you are seeking from an interview should not be information that is easily available from other sources.

Call for an Interview a Few Weeks in Advance

Track down the person's business telephone number; but before you call to request an interview, write out a script, which is the equivalent of a sales pitch. State exactly why you want the interview, and be prepared to explain or give further details if necessary.

Be Persistent

Usually a number of phone calls are involved to secure an interview. Often it takes a couple of weeks to get a date set. Be polite but don't be too quick to take no for an answer. Keep negotiating until you find an opening, even if it means conducting your interview on the telephone.

☐ Before the Interview

Do Your Homework

Before you show up at the interview, find out as much as you can about the subject you will be discussing and about the person you're planning to interview as well. Having this information in advance will show the person that you were interested enough to do some homework ahead of time, and it will save both of you time for the serious questions.

Prepare a List of Questions

- **Arrange your questions in order of priority.** Ask your major questions early in the interview; that way, should the interview get cut short, you will still have gotten important information. Also have a few backup questions handy to keep the flow of talk going on the major topic.

- **Keep your questions few and specific.** Somewhere between eight and twelve questions are usually plenty. Avoid questions that can be answered simply with a yes or no.

- **Prepare a problem/solution question.** Often a good question to ask your interviewee is what he or she sees as the major problem in this particular field or situation and what might be some possible solutions to the problem.

- **End the interview with a good question.** You can close the interview by asking questions that can lead you to further information. For example, "Can you think of any other people I should interview or specific books or articles I should read?"

☐ Conducting the Interview

Tape Record the Interview if Possible

If you plan to tape the interview, ask permission ahead of time; make sure your machine is in good working order and that you have at least two tapes. Recording the interview will take pressure off you and keep you more relaxed and able to focus on getting your questions answered.

Take Notes

Even if you record the interview, take brief notes during the interview as a reminder of the sequence of the conversation. In any case, don't let the writing distract you too much.

Take Down Direct Quotations

Write down some of the exact words and sentences your interviewee says, and put quotation marks around them. Be as accurate as possible when attributing words to another person.

Listen More than You Talk

Relax, keep your ears open, and be a good audience for your interviewee. Don't be afraid of silences and pauses. They allow for on-the-spot thinking.

Take Charge of Ending the Interview

Once you feel you have gotten most of your questions answered, make a cordial but efficient end to the interview. A good way to end the interview before leaving is to ask permission to call and clarify points and information if necessary.

◻ After the Interview Get It Down on Paper Immediately

Write Down Your Thoughts and Impressions

As soon as possible after the interview, jot down some important notes you may not have had time to write. Fill in the gaps in your notes. Also write your evaluation of the interview and the most important piece of information you obtained.

Transcribe Your Tape and Type Up Your Notes

Leave plenty of white space so you can go back and add things you remember later. If you're unsure of some points, call your interviewee for clarification.

Send Your Interviewee a Short Thank-You Note

If you are writing an article or paper based on the interview, offer to send a copy at a later date if that seems appropriate.

CHAPTER 19

DEVISING A SIMPLE SURVEY
(TO GATHER A RANGE OF OPINIONS)

Often you can add another dimension to your research by testing the opinion of other students or members of your community.

Unlike an interview, a survey is not a conversation, so you have to make it easy for people to answer a set list of questions quickly. Like an interview, it's very important to begin your survey from a base of your own information. You should already be familiar with the statistics or other pertinent facts that are available before you undertake a survey.

☐ DECIDE WHAT YOU WANT TO FIND OUT

• What important statistic or other specific piece of information do you want to find out?

• What related information will you need to know beforehand?

☐ DECIDE ON THE PEOPLE YOU WILL SURVEY

Choose thoughtfully the people you will survey, and keep the number of people realistic. You may not have the time and skills to do a thoroughly scientific survey, but you can model your survey on one that professional researchers devise by having a random and broad selection of respondents. For example, you can reasonably expect that your fellow classmates in Freshman English represent a cross-section of students who are taking that course at your college, especially if yours is a general class section that was registered randomly from the student population.

☐ Develop Your Survey

Limit the Number of Questions You Ask

Usually a maximum of eight to ten questions will assure cooperation from busy people.

Don't ask personal information (such as age, religious affiliation, employment status, and the like), unless it is relevant to what you hope to discover.

Refine Your Questions to Yield Short Answers

Simplify your questions wherever possible. This will make compiling results much easier. Make some choices as simple as "true/false," "yes/no," or "agree on a scale of 1–5—with 5 being highest." Anticipate possible answers such as "not applicable." However, leave room on your survey form for comments. You might get a new idea or a quotable remark.

Arrange Your Questions

Arrange your questions with the easiest-to-answer first, and build to more difficult ones. Decide whether your survey needs to be oral or written. Even if it is oral, you will need a standardized form to keep track of the answers.

Anticipate Problems in Getting Honest Answers

Alfred Kinsey, who interviewed people about their sexual habits, discovered years ago that people do not always respond frankly to surveys and often give the expected answer rather than their honest one. If you plan to ask highly sensitive questions, ask them on paper, assure anonymity, and select your respondents in a very open setting, such as a mall.

Test the Form with a Friend

Ask your friend to first answer the questions with his or her own phrasing and then with the choices you have written. Simplify any ambiguous or two-part answers, and eliminate any questions that don't work or are confusing.

◻ DESCRIBE YOUR METHODS WHEN YOU REPORT YOUR RESULTS

Indicate when, where, and how your survey was conducted. Include the number of people questioned and the general population that they represent. Begin your report with the time and place: "A survey of students leaving the college library between 9 and 10 P.M. on Tuesday, November 17, 1998. . . ."

CHAPTER 20

In a Crunch 3
(Limit Your Search)

At this stage, you no longer have the luxury of browsing the Internet, checking out unusual sources, or conducting interviews. Your best shot now is to limit your search to print sources in the library.

☐ Stick to Main Avenues for Information

Use the *Reader's Guide to Periodical Literature* and the *New York Times Index* as your main avenues for locating a few major articles. Use the library catalog to find a few books.

☐ Balance Your Sources

Find more articles than books; make sure that you have a number of recent sources and that you balance introductory and more advanced sources.

☐ Select a Chapter from a Book

Instead of reading a whole book, get several books and use one or two chapters—or an introduction or a conclusion from each.

☐ Don't Get Lost on the Internet

If you're not fairly expert with doing research on the Internet, stay away from it. That's not to say you *can't* use the Internet at the last minute, especially if you're experienced at surfing through it. Just don't lose your focus at the final hour.

PART 4

TELLING WHAT YOU'VE LEARNED

CHAPTER 21

Making a Plan
(Taming Your Information)

You've collected all sorts of information. You have a folder, maybe even a box, full of notes. Now you have to decide what to share with the reader. Are you going to just hand the reader the box? You need to make some decisions, to discover what matters most to you about your research. Then you can build your notes into a unified paper with a clear progression of ideas.

☐ Three Cardinal Rules for Organization

- Make sure that each general statement will be backed up with facts, examples, or logical reasons.

- Let go of any points or bits of information that do not help to show your main ideas; don't include something just because you found an article about it or just because you think it's interesting.

- One method of organization you should always avoid: Do not cover each of your sources one at a time.

☐ Assess Your Sources of Information

Look over all your notes. Categorize them by topic. See whether you have enough to meet the requirements of the assignment. Consider what other information you will need to explain or prove your ideas. But before you begin incorporating material, do a quick check of each source to determine whether or not it is appropriate for your particular topic and paper.

- Rank sources from most useful to least useful, and eliminate the ones that don't add substantially to your information.

- Review your notes from each source you plan to use. Identify the main points each makes. Do a follow-up search if necessary to fill in any missing information.

- Briefly outline the conclusions made by each source you plan to use. How do these support or dispute your own conclusions?

☐ FREEWRITE TO DISCOVER YOUR OWN VIEWPOINT

Your goal in freewriting at this stage is to decide what is important in the material you've found. Set your books and notes aside. Write for twenty minutes without any long pauses. If you run dry, reread what you've written and expand upon one of your points.

As you freewrite, keep these three questions in mind:

- How does what I've learned tie in with what I thought when I started?

- Out of all I've learned, what is most important?

- What does my reader probably know already, and what will I need to explain or prove?

After twenty minutes, go back and underline the most important sentences, the ones that seem to contain your strongest opinions, feelings, and attitudes.

Once you have isolated some good ideas, write a sentence that begins, "The major point I am trying to make in this paper is . . . ." This sentence should clearly state your main *purpose* for your paper. Keep this purpose in front of you as you plan and write your essay.

☐ THREE OPTIONS FOR MAKING A PLAN

Most of us have been taught that the best way to organize is to make an outline and then follow it. This method works for some writers, but many writers prefer instead to strike out and write before stopping to think about organization. There is no one best way to organize.

Write First and Organize Later

With this method, you discover your organization through the process of writing. As you write, don't try to include all the facts from your notes. Don't worry about perfection. Just get down your ideas. Keep going *without starting over* until you reach the end.

When your ideas are all written, go back, read your notes, and decide which information will support each idea.

If this method suits you, remember that you will need to reorganize later in the writing process, cutting repetitions, moving main points, filling gaps.

Write a Very Short First Draft

With this method, write the key assertions you want to prove—all in one paragraph. You should have between four and eight points that are generalizations, not specific facts.

Review your paragraph to make sure it flows smoothly and doesn't repeat the same idea two ways. Then take each of the sentences from your paragraph and make it the first sentence of a page. Go through your notes and decide which facts, quotations, and reasons will go under each sentence.

Now consider rearranging your paper. You may want to move one of the pages to make a better flow, combine two, or cut one.

Start with a Working Outline

With this method, you make a list—in random order—of the key points you have in mind. Then survey your research notes for evidence that will support and clarify each point.

Now play with the arrangement of your points. You may want to drop some and combine others.

From this rough plan, you can proceed to a working outline that lists your main points with minor points and evidence listed under each of them. Remember, you cannot include everything you learned without creating a chaotic paper. Instead, select the information that best demonstrates your key points.

If you need to make a formal or sentence outline, use the traditional system of numbers and letters to show which ideas are parts of other ideas and which facts support particular generalizations. Use *Roman numerals* for the first level, *capital letters* for the second level, *Arabic numerals* for the third level, and *lowercase letters* for the fourth level. At any level you must have at least *two* items. Each point should be stated in a complete sentence.

I. _____
   A. _____
      1. _____
         a. _____
         b. _____
      2. _____
   B. _____
II. _____

A good sentence outline is nearly a first draft of your paper.

☐ REMEMBER YOUR READER

In planning what to include, bear in mind what your reader already knows and what you are explaining that might be new to your reader. Are some explanations unnecessary? Do some terms need to be clarified? Above all, are you trying to persuade your reader of a central point? If so, what are your most persuasive facts and arguments?

☐ TURN YOUR PLAN UPSIDE DOWN

You might have a good plan but still not be satisfied with the organization of your paper. If so, open your mind to the possibility of a radical change of emphasis that makes your paper more exciting to you.

- Perhaps one part of your paper should become the whole paper and the other parts be dropped or subordinated.

- Perhaps you'd be better off to condense background information drastically.

- Perhaps you're covering the same information in two places and should cut one whole section.

■ COMPOSE A THESIS SENTENCE

Having played with the arrangement of your ideas and seen what you really want to stress, you are ready to write a thesis sentence. Take the sentence that you wrote after freewriting, and see if it is still your main point. Write several versions until you have a sentence that sums up your overall point.

Here are thesis sentences that go with the two student papers in the Appendix:

> Sleeping pills—widely overprescribed—are not the answer to sleep deprivation because they do little to help, and their side effects, which include addiction, can be very harmful.

> Today, we take for granted a simple shower or bath with soap and fresh clean water, but in the past keeping clean was not quite so simple.

Your thesis sentence may be complex, but it should not simply be a list of topics your paper will cover.

CHAPTER 22

TRADITIONAL PATTERNS OF ORGANIZATION

(USING A FORMULA)

If you're having a tough time finding an organization for your topic, you may want to see if your material fits one of the following patterns. The danger in using formulas is that they sometimes produce bland, boring papers. If you decide to use one of these patterns, you'll have to work extra hard at keeping your paper lively.

☐ COMPARISON

With this pattern, simply show how things are alike or different. Or use a combination of both to show how things are both alike and different. Keep your comparison within the field itself; going outside your subject field will mean double research for you. Possibilities for this formula are papers that compare two historical eras, two major figures, or two beliefs. A similar pattern is to present the pros and cons of a position.

☐ CHRONOLOGICAL ORDER

This pattern organizes material by time, moving either from the past forward to the present or from the hindsight of the present to the past. You must, however, select and subordinate details to give climactic interest; otherwise your paper will be monotonous. This pattern of development is useful for presenting biographical or historical studies, or for tracing a movement or trend. You can also use this pattern to describe your own growth in awareness as you conducted your research, if the assignment allows you to do so.

☐ PROBLEM AND SOLUTION

This pattern is well suited to current topics (social issues, diseases, fitness, government policy) where you describe an ongoing problem, analyze the various solutions that experts have proposed, and make your own judgment as to the best solution.

☐ CAUSE AND EFFECT

In this pattern you can emphasize either the *causes* or the *effects* and explain the links between them. For example, you might demonstrate how a single government regulation (the cause) has brought about numerous legal loopholes (the effects). Or you might enumerate the reasons (the causes) for the decline of the inner city in America (the effect).

☐ DEFINITION AND EXAMPLE

In this pattern, first present what you have learned about the meaning of a particular term or concept. Do not use the dictionary definition; instead, provide your own definition derived from your research. Then present examples that explain the meaning. This pattern is particularly good for case studies in psychology, medicine, law, or the arts. For example, you could define your understanding of the term *film noir* and then follow with studies of several representative films.

☐ PROCESS

This pattern breaks down your subject into steps of a process, telling how something is made or done. For example, you might explain how to convert a building from using fossil energy to using solar energy, or you might analyze the steps that led to the breakup of the Soviet Union. The challenge in writing a process paper is deciding how much detail is needed: If you tell too little, your reader can't follow you; if you tell too much, your reader gets bored or lost.

☐ Classification

A classification pattern divides a topic into several divisions such as types, major parts, historical divisions, or groups. Some topics that lend themselves to this pattern are types of treatment for a disease, the subsidiaries of a corporation, or groups that make up a political movement.

☐ Argument

With this method, you start by taking a strong position on a controversial issue. The issue can be one that the public is already aware of, or you can present a controversial issue that you feel needs to be more widely known. Give your reasons, one by one, for your point of view and marshal evidence to prove your thesis. A related approach is to begin by presenting several arguments against your position and then refute them one by one.

CHAPTER 23

YOUR FIRST DRAFT
(WRITING WITHOUT YOUR NOTES)

If you try to write your final paper in one draft, you put yourself under too much pressure to make everything perfect the first time around. To make the whole research paper more manageable, approach it in several stages, each time adding information and making adjustments.

■ FOUR CONCERNS YOU CAN DEFER UNTIL LATER

Right away you can put off worrying about four aspects of your paper:

- **The perfect introduction.** Once you see how your paper comes out, you can go back and improve your introduction.

- **Spelling and punctuation.** Save this concern until the revision stage.

- **Documentation.** You will add this information to your second draft.

- **Length.** You don't have to aim for a certain length yet. When you have a full first draft on paper, you'll begin to see where information and explanations are needed.

■ GETTING DOWN A QUICK FIRST DRAFT

In your first draft of the paper, get down your main ideas in order, explaining each one. It's important during this stage not to lose track of what initially motivated you to go with this topic. Therefore, keep your purpose clearly in mind as you write your first draft.

WRITE WITHOUT YOUR NOTES

Start your first draft without your notes in front of you. Put all your notes and books into a closet, and don't refer to them until you've produced a complete first draft. This method forces you to pull together what you've found out and to write it in your own voice and style, rather than to be overly influenced by your notes. You will also be avoiding the worst kind of research paper—one composed mostly of chunks taken from books and articles.

WRITE YOUR FIRST DRAFT IN ONE SITTING

If at all possible, write your first full draft, all the way to your conclusion, in one sitting. Then give yourself a few hours or a day away from the work before you begin your next draft.

◼ AIM YOUR PAPER RIGHT AT YOUR AUDIENCE

Judge the expertise of your audience. Are you writing for a general reader or for an expert in the field? Usually, even when writing for a teacher, you cannot assume a lot of detailed knowledge. On the other hand, don't pad your paper with information that everybody knows.

You will have to guide your reader:

- What will the reader need to know first?
- What terms will need explanation?
- What concerns might the reader already have?

Engage your reader as completely as you can. Anticipate your reader's questions and arguments. In general, put yourself in your reader's place.

☐ WRITE WITH A STRONG VOICE

Adopt a confident tone as you write. Remember that through research you have become somewhat of an authority on this subject. Write your paper from the position of this authority. State your case logically, objectively, and strongly.

Use a straightforward style not very different from the style of other writing you have done. Don't fall into the trap of writing in a phony, artificial style just because this is a research paper.

Using *I* in your paper

Although some teachers may not allow you to use *I* in your papers, using it deliberately in places can be very effective. Using *I* can lead you to a strong and natural writing voice, even if you later decide to delete it in a more formal paper. *I* is appropriate in your introduction when you state your angle on the topic and the thesis you have reached; it is appropriate in the middle of your paper when you evaluate evidence or include any examples from experience; and it is appropriate in your conclusion when you make judgments about the value of what you have learned. This does not mean that you will fill your paper with "I think" and "in my opinion." These phrases are unnecessary and merely clutter your paper.

☐ YOUR PRELIMINARY TITLE

Your title is an announcement of the content of your paper. Therefore, it has to be specific so the reader knows the paper's subject. If your title is too broad, it will be misleading—your reader would expect a book. Instead of a broad title such as "Nursing Homes," use a more specific title such as "The Rising Cost of Nursing Homes in Oklahoma."

Your title is also an advertisement for your paper; it says, "Read me." Therefore, your title should have punch. A title like "Family Stress" can easily be turned into something catchier, such as "Stress—It's All in the Family."

You now have a straightforward version of your paper but without many of the details. Your first draft is not yet a research paper. The next step is to fill in the details from your research.

CHAPTER 24

YOUR SECOND DRAFT

(INCORPORATING INFORMATION FROM YOUR SOURCES)

Once you have a first draft that gets your most important points down on paper, the next step is to add in the facts, quotations, and other evidence that will make your points convincing.

☐ USE A COMPUTER

You may have written your first draft on a computer. If not, it would be a good idea to type it in now and store it for revision. The computer will allow you to insert quotations, facts, and documentation right into your first draft, as well as allow you to make corrections without having to retype.

Reminders

- Never turn off your machine without saving any changes and storing your updated work on a disk.

- Don't erase deletions. Move them to the last page of your document for possible later use.

☐ SEARCH YOUR FIRST DRAFT FOR STATEMENTS THAT NEED SUPPORT

You may need to add information or cut an irrelevant fact. Look for:

- Unsupported generalizations

- Gaps—missing steps, unclear explanations

- Terms that may be unclear

- Necessary background information
- Points that your reader might doubt

▣ RAID YOUR NOTES FOR FACTS AND QUOTATIONS

Reread your notes and select the facts, quotations, and other information that you need to support the various parts of your paper. Make a note on your first draft of where each piece of information will go. As you review your notes, don't get pulled off course by material that seems interesting or significant but that doesn't fit clearly into one of your paragraphs.

▣ INCORPORATE DOCUMENTED INFORMATION GRACEFULLY

Now weave facts, quotations, and opinions of experts into your paper. A good research paper is not just a compilation of information from books, articles, and other sources. You must always stress your perspective, your sequence of ideas.

One big challenge in writing a paper based on research is incorporating your source material into your essay in an inviting way. Nothing is duller than a dull research paper. A good documented paper reads more like a persuasive, interesting essay than a required research paper. Your voice, not the voices of your sources, must control the paper.

- Don't write your paper with a book open next to you, going back and forth from the book to your paper, changing just a few words. Close the book and write the important point in plain English, in your own words.
- Don't overload your paragraphs with facts and quotations.
- Explain or react to information when you present it so that you won't have huge blocks of quotations or an uninterrupted series of citations.

- Alternate between using direct quotation, paraphrase, and summary. Use all three of these in a balanced way throughout your paper.

■ Document Your Sources

As you insert information from your sources into your paper, you also need to tell exactly where the information came from. In your finished paper you will need to indicate the specific page where you found information—facts, quotations, opinions—even if you put that information in your own words. So as you work on your second draft, adding in material from your notes, be sure to include the source and the page number.

CHAPTER 25

USING DIRECT QUOTATIONS
(KEEP THEM FEW AND BRIEF)

You have three options in presenting information gained from books and other sources: *direct quotation, paraphrase,* and *summary.* Inexperienced students tend to quote large blocks of information, but by mixing direct quotation with paraphrase and summary and by weaving in your own comments, your paper will become more truly your own rather than a patchwork of pieces from your sources.

Direct quotations are any exact wording that you take from a source, whether the original source was written or oral.

Use direct quotations to:

• Repeat word for word a memorable statement of opinion

• Present precisely what someone has said so that you can comment on it

Do not use direct quotation to:

• Present facts, statistics, or steps in a process

• Refer to standard terminology in a field

How To Use Direct Quotations Effectively

Quotations should make up no more than fifteen percent of your paper. Most of the words and ideas in the paper should be your own; use the words and opinions of others only to support the points you are making. Don't let your sources' words dominate your paper.

Keep the quotations short. It's tempting to use big blocks of information, especially when the information is well written. Resist this temptation. You can quote complete sentences at times, sometimes even two sentences, but seldom more.

Incorporate fragments of direct quotations into your own sentences.   A graceful (and easy) way to quote is to use just a word or a phrase from your source, worked smoothly into your own sentence. Make certain that your sentence is complete and that it makes sense.

> Medical treatment of racehorses has changed in recent years, becoming "misdirected from the art of healing to the craft of portfolio management" (Ferraro 8).*

Similarly, you can use your own commentary to link quotations.

> W. E. B. DuBois considered folk songs "the greatest gift of the Negro people" to American culture; in fact, he claims that they are "the most beautiful expression of human experience born this side [of] the seas" (182).

Comment on each quotation.   In general, do not begin or end a paragraph with a direct quotation. State your point clearly before you use a quotation, and after you've quoted it, make a comment about it. Ask yourself, What's the point of this quotation? Make that point clear to your reader.

> East Africa is increasingly plagued by mass hunger that continues to be bred by overpopulation, crop failure, and wars. Jonathan Stevenson says, "There are no meccas in East Africa, only shifting places of refuge for starving and uprooted people" (16), and these "places of refuge" are often impossible to reach.

Weave your sources together.   Don't have a block of quotations from one source in a part of your paper and then all the quotations from another source somewhere else. Instead, weave the quotations together.

> In various parts of the world, fish hatcheries are allowing some of their fish to escape and to spread disease to wild fish. Laurie MacBride describes "new parasites and diseases" (26) occurring in the Georgia Bay of Ontario. Stephen Cline reports on a similar problem "traced to a hatchery" (36) in Norway. The

Parenthetical citations of page numbers in this chapter refer to sources listed in the Works Cited page at the end of this chapter.

problem is further aggravated, as Marcia Barinaga points out, because antibiotics used in hatcheries eventually "promote the growth of antibiotic-resistant bacteria" in the ocean (630).

Clearly identify each quotation.   Never leave quotations dangling in your paper. Always make clear who is speaking.

Copy the quotation exactly.   Retain the writer's spelling and punctuation. Double check to make sure you have not left out anything. If the writer says "I," you must retain the "I" in your quotation.

How To Punctuate Direct Quotations Correctly

When you use another person's words, use the *exact* wording from your material and frame the words with quotation marks. However, if you change the wording, you cannot surround the words with quotation marks.

PUNCTUATION BEFORE QUOTATIONS

Use quotation marks for a few words.   For quotations of one word or a few words, simply incorporate the word or phrase into your sentence and then enclose the word or words in double quotation marks. Use no other punctuation.

> William Irvine considers Thomas Huxley's view of religion to be "negative" (404).

Use a comma to separate a quotation from a tag.   Use a comma after a tag when it introduces a quotation. Use a comma after a quotation when a tag follows it.

> Sharon Mazer says, "Professional wrestling is frequently criticized as a crude, brutal sport that lacks even the honesty of competition" (97).

> "Professional wrestling is frequently criticized as a crude, brutal sport that lacks even the honesty of competition," says Sharon Mazer (97).

However, use no comma when you use *that.*

Sharon Mazer says that "professional wrestling is frequently criticized as a crude, brutal sport that lacks even the honesty of competition" (97).

Use a colon to set off quotations of one or two sentences.   Usually you make a full statement before the colon, and the quotation illustrates that statement. Do not use tags such as "he says" when you use a colon.

Ron Matou describes the universal symbolism of mountain-climbing: "Mountaineering is one of the ways in which the human spirit has aspired to transcend its physical limitations" (10).

PUNCTUATION WITHIN QUOTATIONS

Use brackets to indicate that a word has been changed or added. Sometimes a quotation taken out of context is not completely clear and you need to change or explain a word. If so, place your words in brackets.

An article in *Popular Mechanics* tells how "the FSX [Future Shock Experimental—a new bicycle] also has cable-activated hydraulic disc brakes similar to those used on motorcycles" ("Bike" 100).

Use ellipsis to indicate words left out.   Often you want to quote only part of a statement. Perhaps the middle is irrelevant to your point, or you want to omit unnecessary words. Use ellipsis marks (three periods separated by spaces) within brackets to indicate you have left out material. Use a fourth period outside the bracket to end your sentence.

In explaining Winston Churchill's determination to become a great orator, James Humes reveals that Churchill "suffered from a habitual stutter [. . .] and also had a congenital lisp" (44).

Use single quotation marks for a quotation within a quotation. When you quote someone who is quoting someone else, you then have a quotation within a quotation. Simply use single quotation marks (the apostrophe mark) for the second speaker.

Jerome Bruner points out that narrative "must be concrete: it must 'ascend to the particular,' as Karl Marx put it" (60).

Use *sic* to indicate an error that belongs to your source, not to you. If there is a mistake in a quotation you need to use, reprint the error exactly, but right after it add *sic* (in brackets), which means that you have reproduced the error as you found it.

> Analyzing the art of quilting, Patricia Mainardi says that "Time seems to be the principle [sic] ingredient in traditional quilts" (52).

PUNCTUATION AFTER QUOTATIONS

Place periods and commas inside the closing quotation marks.

> The Bible advises us to "turn the other cheek."

> When Greta Garbo said, "I want to be alone," she really meant it.

However, if a parenthesis follows a quotation, put the period after the closing parenthesis, as in several of the examples on this page.

Place semicolons outside the closing quotation marks.

> Alfred Kazin, in assessing the impact of photography on our culture, says that "the visual has become our immediate world, our everyday environment"; however, he goes on to say that the excessive use of visuals today often has a deadening effect (35).

Place most question marks and exclamation points inside.

> "What did he know and when did he know it?" was the most quoted line from the hearings.

However, if *you* are asking or exclaiming, the mark goes *outside*.

> What did Joyce Cary mean when he wrote that genius is "much more fragile than talent"? (51).

INDENTING LONG QUOTATIONS

Quotations of four or more lines must be set off by indenting each line ten spaces from the left margin. Do not use quotation marks.

If the quotation is a complete sentence, end it with a period, before the parenthesis.

Stephen Nachmanovitch says that improvisation happens not just in the arts, but also in everyday conversation:

> As we talk and listen, we are drawing on a set of building blocks (vocabulary) and rules for combining them (grammar). These have been given to us by our culture. But the sentences we make with them may never have been said before and may never be said again. Every conversation is a form of jazz. (17)

After the quotation, return to the left margin and discuss what was important in the quotation.

Works Cited in This Chapter

Barinaga, Marcia. "Fish, Money, and Science in Puget Sound." *News and Comment* 9 Feb. 1990: 631.

"Bike to the Future." *Popular Mechanics* Aug. 1992: 100–1.

Bruner, Jerome. *Acts of Meaning*. Cambridge: Harvard UP, 1990.

Cary, Joyce. *Art and Reality: Ways of the Creative Process*. New York: Harper, 1958.

Cline, Stephen. "Down on the Fish Farm." *Sierra* Mar.–Apr. 1989: 34–38.

DuBois, W. E. B. *The Souls of Black Folk*. New York: Washington Square, 1970.

Ferraro, Gregory. "The Corruption of Nobility: Rise and Fall of Thoroughbred Racing in America." *The North American Review* May–June 1992: 4–8.

Humes, James C. "Churchill on the Stump." *Civilization* Jan. 1996: 44–45.

Irvine, William. *Apes, Angels & Victorians*. New York: Time, 1963.

Kazin, Alfred. "Ours Is a Visual Period." *Doubletake* Spring 1997: 31–35.

MacBride, Laurie. "Alliance Fights for Georgia Strait." *Canadian Dimension* Oct. 1990: 24–27.

Mainardi, Patricia. "Quilt Survivals and Revivals." *Arts Magazine* May 1988: 49–57.

Matou, Ron. "Quest for the Summit." *Parabola* Winter 1992: 10–15.

Mazer, Sharon. "The Doggie Doggie World of Professional Wrestling." *The Drama Review* 34 (Winter 1990): 96–122.

Nachmanovitch, Stephen. *Free Play: The Power of Improvisation in Life and the Arts*. Los Angeles: Tarcher, 1990.

Stevenson, Jonathan. "Food for Naught." *The New Republic* 21 Sept. 1992: 13+.

CHAPTER 26

USING PARAPHRASE

(RELATE INFORMATION IN YOUR OWN WORDS)

To *paraphrase*, you take someone else's words and put them into your own words. You reword a statement completely and restate another person's ideas. If you can paraphrase an idea, then you know you have grasped it. The challenge in paraphrasing is to capture the exact sense of a passage or statement without using the same words. You put the information into your own words; it should sound like you.

Don't forget: Paraphrased material must be documented the same as direct quotation. You must acknowledge your source of information.

Use Paraphrase to:

• Report a series of facts

• Write in your own voice and style instead of overquoting

• Use information that is not necessarily written in an interesting or concise manner

• Bring technical information down to an easy reading level

• Clarify a point—that is, write a paraphrase that is clearer than the original

■ USE PARAPHRASE CORRECTLY

Write Your Paraphrase from Memory

Without consulting your notes, write your paraphrase using your own words; then go back and check for accuracy. This method will keep you from plagiarizing as well as help you see if you understand what you've read.

Distinguish Your Wording from any Direct Quotations

If you need to consult your source while writing from memory, restate everything in your own words. If you incorporate any wording from your source, you are employing *direct quotation* with the paraphrase, so use quotation marks around those words.

Check the Definitions of Any Unusual Words

Look up any unusual words in the dictionary to be certain that you completely understand the passage word for word.

Make Certain Your Paraphrase Can Stand Alone

Your paraphrase should be readable and clear all on its own and should not depend upon reference to your source for clarification.

Identify Your Source within the Paraphrase

As a general rule, you should identify your source by name and area of expertise; include your own judgment of how the source has presented an idea—in other words, provide a slight interpretation.

☐ SAMPLE PARAPHRASES FOR STUDY

Here are two short paraphrases that will give you some ideas for how a paraphrase should be constructed.

The original is taken from Adrienne Rich, *On Lies, Secrets, and Silence: Selected Prose 1966–1978*. New York: Norton, 1979.

> *Original*
>
> When a woman is admitted to higher education—particularly graduate school—it is often made to sound as if she enters a sexually neutral world of "disinterested" and "universal" perspectives. It is assumed that coeducation means the equal

education, side by side, of women and men. Nothing could be further from the truth. (134)

Paraphrase

When women enter graduate school, they harbor the illusion that they are becoming part of a world that will provide them with an education equal to what men get. Not so, warns Adrienne Rich (134).

The original is taken from Loren Eiseley, *The Immense Journey*. New York: Vintage, 1957.

Original

Every so often out of the millions of the human population, a six-year-old child or a teen-age youth dies of old age. The cause of this curious disease, known as progeria, or premature aging, is totally unknown. (108)

Paraphrase

Anthropologist Loren Eiseley reports that premature aging, a strange disease with no known causes, sometimes kills very young people (108).

CHAPTER 27

USING SUMMARY

(WHITTLE DOWN LARGE BLOCKS OF INFORMATION)

Like paraphrase, a *summary* restates someone else's words. When you summarize, you restate an idea in considerably shorter form— *sum it up*—in your own words. You can summarize anything from a paragraph to a complete book.

Don't forget: Summarized material, just like direct quotations and paraphrases, must be documented. You must acknowledge your source of information.

Use summary to:

• Acknowledge a conflicting idea

• Introduce a related idea without too much detail

• Cover a large amount of material in a few words

■ USE SUMMARY EFFECTIVELY

Choose Only What Is Essential

Carefully ferret out only the major ideas. Delete extraneous material examples, entertaining passages, or rhetorical statements.

Catch What Is Distinctive about the Writer's Idea

Don't just say "This is a book about baseball." Give the author's point of view: "This is a book about how baseball has changed since the 1970s."

Summarize Sequentially

Take down the ideas in the order in which they were written. When you present the ideas, you may sometimes want to rearrange the points for greater emphasis, but it is usually better to summarize in the author's sequence of ideas.

Stick Closely to the Text

Condense only the ideas you have read. Do not add anything new. A summary is not the place to add your own interpretations.

Identify Your Source within the Summary

Just as you do with paraphrase, identify your source by giving the author's name and area of expertise.

☐ SAMPLE SURVEY FOR STUDY

Here is sample summary. The original is taken from Diane Ackerman, *A Natural History of the Senses*. New York: Random, 1990.

> *Original*
>
> Our skin is what stands between us and the world. If you think about it, no other part of us makes contact with something not us but the skin. It imprisons us, but it also gives us individual shape, protects us from invaders, cools us down or heats us up as need be, produces Vitamin D, holds in our body fluids. Most amazing, perhaps, is that it can mend itself when necessary, and it is constantly renewing itself. Weighing from six to ten pounds, it's the largest organ of the body, and the key organ of sexual attraction. Skin can take a startling variety of shapes: claws, spines, hooves, feathers, scales, hair. It's waterproof, washable, and elastic. Although it may cascade or roam as we grow older, it lasts surprisingly well. For most cultures, it's the ideal canvas to decorate with paints, tattoos, and jewelry. But, most of all, it harbors the sense of touch. (68)

Summary

Diane Ackerman, in *A Natural History of the Senses*, describes skin basically as a container which keeps us separate from the rest of the world. Our largest organ, it constantly heals and renews itself. Best of all, skin, as our only contact with the world, supplies us with our sense of touch (68).

A general summary of Ackerman's whole book might go like this:

In *A Natural History of the Senses*, Diane Ackerman employs a personal narrative style as a way to draw the reader into a very sophisticated discussion of the origin and evolution of the five senses. The book is scientific, cross-cultural, and entertaining. In her thorough explorations of smell, touch, taste, hearing, and vision, Ackerman maintains that it is through our senses that we "make sense" of our lives.

CHAPTER 28

Incorporating Illustrations

(Adding Visual Information to Your Paper)

We take for granted how much we depend on illustrations in our daily reading, yet few college papers use them. Most papers can be enhanced with the use of a well-chosen illustration or two; and some topics, such as graphic arts or technical subjects, cannot be adequately explained without them.

Illustrations can range from charts and graphs to drawings, diagrams, and photographs. You can photocopy them from other sources, so long as you give copyright information, or you can create visuals yourself. Computers make creating graphics fun and easy.

Here are a few ideas to guide you if you decide to use illustrations:

- **Make sure each illustration has a purpose for being in the paper.** Don't just stick in an illustration for visual effect. Use it to give additional information or to clarify information.

- **Keep it simple.** Each visual should communicate one idea.

- **Give each visual a commentary right beneath it.** Explain what you want your reader to understand.

- **Place visuals into the text right at the point they support or in an appendix at the end.**

- **Give the source of the illustration.** See page 123.

Be sure that all of your illustrations are clear and that they are securely fastened into your paper.

CHAPTER 29

IN A CRUNCH 4

(PULLING A PAPER TOGETHER)

☐ TAKE ONE STEP AT A TIME—EVEN UNDER PRESSURE

No matter how pressed you are for time, control your panic and work in sequential stages. You may think that doing several steps instead of one big one will take too much time; but in fact, by reducing the mental pressure, working in stages will save time as well as improve the final result.

☐ MAKE A BRIEF PLAN

Jot down several ideas that you can present in a paper and then arrange them in a reasonable order. These few items can serve as your outline. If you can't come up with any ideas for a plan, check Chapter 22, "Traditional Patterns of Organization," for help.

☐ WRITE A QUICK FIRST DRAFT WITHOUT YOUR NOTES

Before you begin your draft, spend ten minutes freewriting to discover your main emphasis. Then begin writing your draft in one sitting, using plain English. At this point, don't stop to check your notes or worry about spelling or exact phrasing or missing facts.

☐ INCORPORATE FACTS AND QUOTATIONS

Look through your rough draft for the points you want to expand or verify with information from your sources. Don't add too many facts or quotations. Keep it clear and simple, and use only what is necessary to make your main points understandable. Don't overquote. Tell facts in your own words.

◻ TAKE CHARGE OF WRITER'S BLOCK

If you find yourself completely stuck, take charge of your block by talking to someone else about your topic. Get some ideas stirring in your head and then freewrite. Keep responding to a simple question: What matters to me most about this subject?

PART 5

DOCUMENTATION: GIVING CREDIT TO YOUR SOURCES

CHAPTER 30

PLAGIARISM

(DON'T STEAL OTHER PEOPLE'S IDEAS)

Plagiarism means you have presented other people's facts, ideas, or words as if they were your own—whether you did so deliberately, carelessly, or unconsciously.

- You must give credit to all sources of information.

- Material must be credited whether the wording was copied (and thus must be surrounded by quotation marks) or put in your own words.

■ GUIDELINES FOR AVOIDING PLAGIARISM

- Do not use someone else's phrasing without quotation marks. Although standard terminology in a field does not get quotation marks—for example, chronic fatigue syndrome—you still document the source.

- Do not use someone else's idea, date, or statistic without telling specifically where you found it.

- Do not collaborate with a friend to the extent that your friend dictates the ideas or phrasing of your paper.

- Do not hand in a paper that you have written for another course without your teacher's consent. Some teachers consider this to be another form of plagiarism. Of course, do not submit someone else's paper or one downloaded from the Internet.

■ THE RISKS

If you hand in a paper that contains someone else's phrasing or ideas without giving credit to that person, you are taking big risks. If your teacher proves that you have plagiarized, you might fail the course or you might be permanently expelled from the college or university. These punishments have been upheld in court.

It is easy for a teacher to spot plagiarism in a student paper. Even in a large class where the teacher may not know each student's style, the teacher will recognize the style of professional sources in the field and may even be extremely familiar with the sources you have used.

There is a risk of unconscious plagiarism. After immersing yourself in your research project, you may acquire a whole new vocabulary you have never used before. Technical terms and phrases that are common to a particular field do not have to be documented. However, be extremely careful not to adopt another person's ideas or distinctive phrases—no matter how popular or often-quoted—without using quotation marks and a parenthetical citation.

☐ Examples of Plagiarism

Imagine that you are writing a paper about the uses of Greek mythology in the poetry of Percy Bysshe Shelley and one of your sources is the first paragraph in Thomas Bulfinch's *The Age of Fable, or Beauties of Mythology*. William H. Klapp, ed. New York: Tudor, 1935.

> The religions of ancient Greece and Rome are extinct. The so-called divinities of Olympus have not a single worshipper among living men. They belong now not to the department of theology, but to those of literature and taste. There they still hold their place, and will continue to hold it, for they are too closely connected with the finest productions of poetry and art, both ancient and modern, to pass into oblivion. (Bulfinch 1)

Deliberate Plagiarism—Direct Copying of the Original

> Although there is not a single living worshipper of the Greek or Roman gods, they will never pass into oblivion because they are too closely connected with the finest productions of poetry and art.

This sample should be totally revised, either to quote Bulfinch accurately or to paraphrase him. Either revision would still need to give credit to Bulfinch.

Careless Plagiarism—Use of the Original Idea and a Rearrangement and Minor Modification of the Phrasing

The Greek and Roman gods' close connection to the finest productions of poetry and art assure their continued place in civilization.

This sentence needs to be rephrased in the student's own words or put back in Bulfinch's exact phrases and then surrounded by quotation marks. Either variation will still need to be credited to Bulfinch.

Unconscious Plagiarism

Even though no one believes in them today, I think that the Greek and Roman gods will always be important because they have inspired so much great art and literature.

Here the judgment—although not the phrasing—is from Bulfinch who must be given credit for it.

◻ CORRECTING PLAGIARISM

You can correct plagiarism with either quotation, paraphrase, or summary.

Quotation

The Greek and Roman gods, according to Bulfinch, "are too closely connected with the finest productions of poetry and art, both ancient and modern, to pass into oblivion" (1).

Paraphrase

Bulfinch says the Greek and Roman religions continue to influence art and literature even though the believers died long ago (1).

Summary

Bulfinch stresses the lasting influence of Greek and Roman religions on today's art and literature (1).

☐ USING YOUR SOURCES EFFECTIVELY— WITHOUT PLAGIARISM

Whether you quote, summarize, or paraphrase, you always need to document your sources. Not to do so is *plagiarism;* whether *deliberate, careless,* or *unconscious.* Here is how you can prevent plagiarism:

Take notes carefully. Most of the time, put what you read into your own words; write down the source and specific page number for every idea.

Document anything you photocopy. Be sure to write on the photocopy all bibliographical information, including page number.

Be careful when copying material onto your computer disk. Place each section under a different file name, and add source information within the document if the computer program hasn't already done so. Keep your own ideas in a separate file. Immediately place quotation marks around any phrase before importing it into your paper.

Don't count on your memory. When you hear a relevant announcement on the radio, for example, immediately jot down the time, day, and station. Or if you are skimming an article that has only one usable fact, write all the bibliographic information down anyway. You'll be surprised how often such bits of information insist on being used and how hard they are to track down later.

Write the citations as you draft your paper. Place citations immediately into the line after you have used material from your sources. You may later rearrange the paragraph for logic or style, but the credit will be in its proper place.

Don't throw anything away. As you're copying material from your notes into your paper, keep a box handy to store everything until you've completed the project. That way, if you need to give the source for an idea, you can still do so without having to go back to the library.

Proofread your documentation. After you have written the paper, do one last check, comparing notes and source materials to make sure that you haven't inadvertently slipped in a phrase or fact that you haven't given credit for. A good question to ask yourself is, Would the members of my class know this? If the answer is no, then the sentence needs a citation.

CHAPTER 31

PARENTHETICAL CITATION
(*MLA STYLE FOR ENGLISH AND FOREIGN LANGUAGES*)

Documentation is the method that answers your readers' questions: Where did you get this idea? or How do you know that this statistic is true? Documentation provides the sources of your information.

You document the results of your research in two ways:

Citations

Works Cited

Citations are brief references in your text to where you found the information.

The full reference can be found in the Works Cited page at the end of your paper. Citations are covered in this chapter, and Works Cited are covered in the next chapter.

☐ WHY YOU MUST DOCUMENT

When you report the results of your research, you are adding to the work of a community of experts. You document your research:

• To lend authority to your assertions by adding the weight of expert opinion to your evidence

• To allow your readers to explore the subject further

• To avoid plagiarism

☐ WHAT YOU MUST DOCUMENT

Give credit for everything you learned during your research: *facts; statistics;* and *other people's words, ideas, or opinions.*

You must document whether you are quoting or using your own words. However, you do not give a source—even if you learned it during your research—for material that is general knowledge or is an obvious conclusion from the information. For example, you may not have known about the Chicago fire in 1871; you would need to give the source for any details you reported about it, but you wouldn't have to give credit for the fact that Chicago is in Illinois or for the judgment that the fire was devastating.

☐ WHERE YOU MUST DOCUMENT

- The citation must be in the same paragraph where the information is presented.

- Most of the time, the citation is at the end of the sentence.

- The citation may appear midsentence, immediately after information that is unusual or startling or when several facts in the same sentence come from different sources.

☐ HOW OFTEN TO DOCUMENT

When several facts in a row within one paragraph all come from the same page of a source, use one citation to cover them all. Place the citation after the last fact, but alert the reader at the outset with a phrase such as "According to Helen Collins."

Do not, however, wait more than a few lines to let the reader know where the facts came from.

☐ PARENTHETICAL CITATION: FOR ENGLISH CLASSES, THE MLA STYLE

The MLA (Modern Language Association) style is the documentation format used in scholarly publications and courses in English and foreign languages. Other disciplines use different formats, but unless you are given a specific style to follow for papers in an English or literature course, use the MLA style.

This style places the last name of the author and the page number in parentheses immediately after any research information. At the end of the paper, a complete list of sources (Works Cited) provides the titles, dates, and other details about the particular books, articles, and other documents you used. This system has the advantage of naming your sources as you present the information. Its disadvantage is that you have to learn how to punctuate around those parentheses.

General MLA Format for Parenthetical Citations

- Place the last name of the author plus the page number inside parentheses.

  The design of the building blends with the landscape (Stein 69).

- If you have already introduced the author's name, just give the page number in parentheses.

  Wendell Berry defends his resistance to the technology of word processing (67).

- Do not use *p* or *pg* for *page*; just give the number. If the source does not have page numbers, give the number of the section (preceded by sec.), paragraph (para.), or line (l.) if possible.

- For a short quotation or paraphrase incorporated into a line of your paragraph, do not punctuate before the opening parenthesis. Place a period outside the second parenthesis, unless you are continuing your sentence.

  Both boys and girls have masculine and feminine sides (Steinem 257).

- For a long quotation (more than three lines) that is set off (indented ten spaces), end the quotation with a period and then place the citation in parentheses without a period.

  The little boy who is ridiculed for crying "like a girl" doesn't stop feeling sad, he just buries that emotion; and the little girl who is punished for willfulness as a "tomboy" just takes that spirit underground. (Steinem 257)

Special Cases

No author listed   Give the first important word of the title. Underline, italicize, or quote the title as appropriate (see pages 129–30).

Note that it cannot be a word (such as the name of your topic) common to other titles on your Works Cited page; the reader has to be able to recognize your reference. Use several words if necessary.

> The number of single-parent households is declining ("Two-Parent Families" A17).

A quotation that your source has quoted   Identify in your sentence who actually said it or wrote it. Then in your citation use the phrase qtd. in (for "quoted in").

> Scott Eckert has recorded the deep dives of the leatherback turtle, and gives it "a tentative 400-foot lead" over the diving record of the sperm whale (qtd. in "Up Front" 14).

> Linda Sanford and Mary Ellen Donovan say low self-esteem makes a woman "terrified of getting too close" (qtd. in Steinem 259).

An encyclopedia, magazine, or newspaper article   Give the author if listed; if not, then give a brief form of the title of the article; add the page number. Do not give the title of the encyclopedia, magazine, or newspaper.

> One approach is to analyze the Psalms for the richness of their poetic imagery ("Biblical Literature" 842).

A work that has two or three authors   Give all the last names, joined by *and*.

> "A B-type star is an object exhibiting neutral helium lines in its spectrum, but no ionized helium lines" (Jaschek and Jaschek 136).

> Synthesized marijuana is used to treat asthma and to control nausea during chemotherapy (Jaffe, Petersen, and Hodgson 78).

A work that has four or more authors   Give the last name of the first one only, plus et al. ("and others").

> A group of environmental scientists argue that "perpetual Third World poverty is a luxury that the prosperous can no longer afford" (Ehrlich et al. 104).

Two or more works by the same author   Give the author's name, a brief version of the title, and the page number.

> Men and women have different purposes while engaging in conversation (Tannen, *You Just Don't* 77).

An interview or lecture   Do not use a parenthetical citation. Instead, mention the name of the interviewee or speaker and his or her job title and how you heard the information.

> In an interview, Max Sherman, Dean Emeritus of the Lyndon B. Johnson School for Public Affairs at the University of Texas, said that the proposal is worthy of consideration.

Electronic sources   Give enough information in your sentence so the reader will recognize the source in the Works Cited page. Or give the author if listed or the title in parentheses.

> William Wyler's 1939 film presents the moors of Wuthering Heights as a private playground for Catherine and Heathcliff.

> "Deliberative polling" is being used to determine how much customers are willing to pay for clean energy (Green Power Network).

Illustrations or graphics   Give the artist and the page number.

- If the visual illustrates the text with which it appears, give the author or title of the text as well.

> This photograph of the University of California at Santa Cruz illustrates the result of careful environmental planning (Hursley in Stein 72–73).

Note that only Stein (who wrote the article) will be listed in your Works Cited.

- If the visual is independent from any text (such as a cartoon), give only the artist and the page.

> Sometimes, the dog really did eat the homework, as this cartoon illustrates (Levin 56).

Levin, who drew the cartoon, will appear in your Works Cited.

- If the artist is not identified (for instance, in an advertisement) give the author (or owner of the copyright) and page where the illustration appeared.

> This advertisement illustrates the effectiveness of good food photography (Kraft Foods 5).

After you have incorporated the citations of your sources, prepare the last page of your paper, the Works Cited page, as explained in the next chapter. A complete sample paper using parenthetical citations and a Works Cited page according to the MLA style is in the Appendix of this book.

AN EXAMPLE OF PARENTHETICAL CITATION

Sources are listed completely in the Works Cited at the end of this chapter.

> Boys are taught assertiveness (even aggression) at a very young age to prove their masculinity (Keen 38). Girls, however, are brought up to control their aggressive feelings and to prove their femininity by caring about others. Besides being governed by different codes of behavior, according to Deborah Tannen, the sexes "grow up in different worlds of words" (*You Just Don't* 43). The way our society treats girls and boys while they are growing up explains the problems that women and men have in communication (Tannen, *That's Not*). These labels of what is "masculine" or what is "feminine" deny the fact that all human beings have a range of feelings—sometimes needing to connect with others and at other times needing to be independent or dominant. As Gloria Steinem observes:
>
> > The little boy who is ridiculed for crying "like a girl" doesn't stop feeling sad, he just buries that emotion; and the little girl who is punished for willfulness as a "tomboy" just takes that spirit underground. (257)

Notice how these citations have been used; they represent the most common forms:

- The first citation is after a paraphrase; it includes the last name of the author and the page number on which the original information appeared.

- The second citation is after a direct quotation of a phrase. Since the author was mentioned in the sentence, her last name is not given. However, a brief form of the title of her book (underlined or italicized) is given because, as the next citation makes clear, there are two books by this same author.

- The third citation requires the author's name because it has not been given in the sentence. However, the title of the book is also given to distinguish this citation from the one before. When no page is given, you know that the citation is for the whole work—in this case, Tannen's book.

- The last citation is after a direct quotation. The author's name introduced the quotation, so only the page number is needed. This quotation is set off ten spaces because it is longer than three lines.

You will notice that not only direct quotations require documentation. Summaries and paraphrases also require documentation.

Works Cited in This Chapter

Berry, Wendell. "The Body and the Machine." *Parabola* 15 (Fall 1990): 66–74.

"Biblical Literature and Its Critical Interpretation." *Encyclopaedia Britannica: Macropaedia*. 15th ed.

Ehrlich, Paul R., et al. "No Middle Way on the Environment." *Atlantic Monthly* Dec. 1997: 98–104.

Green Power Network. *We Want Clean Energy*. 15 Dec. 1997. United States. Dept. of Energy. 18 Apr. 1998 <http://www.eren.doe.gov/ greenpower/elpaso.html>.

Jaffe, Jerome, Robert Petersen, and Ray Hodgson. *Addictions: Issues and Answers*. New York: Harper, 1980.

Jaschek, Carlos, and Mercedes Jaschek. *The Classification of the Stars*. New York: Cambridge UP, 1987.

Keen, Sam. *Fire in the Belly: On Being a Man*. New York: Bantam, 1991.

Kraft Foods. Advertisement. *Eating Well* July/Aug. 1997: 5.

Levin, Arnie. Cartoon. *New Yorker* 26 May 1997: 56.

Sherman, Max. Dean Emeritus, Lyndon Baines Johnson School of Public Affairs. Telephone Interview. Austin, TX. 21 Sept. 1997.

Stein, Karen. "Two California Campuses." *Architectural Record* 185 (Aug. 1997): 66–75.

Steinem, Gloria. *Revolution from Within*. Boston: Little, Brown, 1992.

Tannen, Deborah. *That's Not What I Meant!* New York: Ballantine, 1986.

---. *You Just Don't Understand: Women and Men in Conversation*. New York: Ballantine, 1990.

"Two-Parent Families Increasing in the U.S." *New York Times* 17 Oct. 1995: A17.

"Up Front: Yertle: 1 Orca: 0." *Discover* Sept. 1987: 14.

Wyler, William. *Wuthering Heights*. Videocassette. CBS Fox, 1939. 118 min.

Note: We have used italics for titles here. Underlining is equally correct, but do not mix the formats.

CHAPTER 32

WORKS CITED
(*MLA* STYLE FOR LISTING YOUR SOURCES)

A Works Cited is a page at the end of your paper that lists all the references (works) you used. Each entry will give the author, title and publisher's information.

A typical Works Cited entry for a book:

> Terkel, Studs. *My American Century*. New York: New Press, 1997.

A typical Works Cited entry for an article:

> Caducci, Bernardo J., and Philip G. Zimbardo. "Are You Shy?" *Psychology Today* Nov./Dec. 1995: 34–40.

◻ MAKING A LIST OF WORKS YOU ACTUALLY CITED

First, go through the entire paper and note the authors or titles of the sources you mentioned when you were reporting the results of your research. Most of those sources will be in parenthetical citations, but be sure to look for sources that do not get parenthetical citations— most electronic sources, people you interviewed, and institutions you visited.

Make a list by writing down the last name of every author you cited or the first main word of the title if no author was listed. If you are using a computer, type up the list and use the computer to alphabetize (usually Sort under Table). Delete any duplications. This is the outline of your Works Cited page.

☐ GENERAL FORMAT
OF THE WORKS CITED PAGE

Formatting details—*arrangement, punctuation,* and *spacing*—are an important part of the formal presentation of academic research, so paying attention to these guidelines may affect the grade of your paper.

- Alphabetize the entire list by the last name of author, editor, artist, or speaker. If no author is given, alphabetize using the first major word of the title. Include *A, An,* or *The,* but do not use them when alphabetizing.

- Do not separate items by type (for example, books and articles), unless asked to do so.

- Do not number the items. Begin each item at the left margin. Continue the first line to the right margin, and then indent the other lines five spaces (or half an inch) from the left margin.

- Double-space the entire list, and do not add extra spaces between items.

- Skip one space after each period, comma, and colon.

- End each entry with a period.

☐ FORMAT FOR AUTHORS' NAMES

One Author   List the last name first, followed by a comma, and then list the first name followed by a period.

> Sagan, Carl. *Billions and Billions: Thoughts on Life and Death on the Brink of the Millenium.* New York: Random, 1997.

Two or Three Authors   Reverse the name of only the first author if there are more than one.

> Burka, Jane B., and Lenora M. Yuen. *Procrastination: Why You Do It, What to Do About It.* Toronto: Addison, 1983.

> Fagen, Richard, Richard Brody, and Thomas O'Leary. *Cubans in Exile.* Stanford, CA: Stanford UP, 1968.

Four or More Authors   List only the first of four or more authors (as given on the title page), followed by the abbreviation et al. (meaning "and others").

> Dennis, Deborah, et al. "A Decade of Research and Services for Homeless Mentally Ill Persons." *American Psychologist* 46 (Nov. 1991): 1129–1138.

Same Author for Two or More Works   List the works alphabetically according to the first main word of each title. Write the author's name for only the first work. *Use three hyphens and a period* in place of the author's name for the second work. Give all other bibliographical information for each work, even if some of the information is the same.

> Wren, Christopher S. "Keeping Cocaine Resilient: Low Cost and High Profit." *New York Times* 4 Mar. 1997: A1, A20.

> ---. "Marijuana Use by Youth Continues to Rise." *New York Times* 20 Feb. 1996: A11.

No Author   If the author is not named, alphabetize by the first main word of the title of the article or booklet.

> "What's Luck Got to Do with It?" *Fortune* 16 Oct. 1995: 148+.

■ FORMAT FOR TITLES

Give the title of the complete work you used.   If you used only one chapter or article in a book, give the author and title of that chapter first, and then give the author and title of the book.

Capitalize the first word and all the main words of the title.   Do so regardless of how the title was capitalized (or not) in the original source.

Italicize or underline with an unbroken line the titles of any work published by itself.   Do so for books; magazines; newspapers; brochures or pamphlets; films; recordings; Web sites; and computer, television, or radio programs. Use the same format throughout your paper.

> Phillips, Adam. *On Kissing, Tickling, and Being Bored: Psychoanalytic Essays on the Unexamined Life.* Cambridge: Harvard UP, 1993.

> *Shot in Hollywood.* Videocassette. Carousel, 1986. 16 min.

Use double quotation marks around the titles of short works.   This applies for pieces published inside larger works, including articles, chapters, stories, essays, poems, songs, and cartoons.

> Newman, Judith. "At Your Disposal: The Funeral Industry Prepares for Boom Times." *Harper's* Nov. 1997: 61–71.

> Wylie, Judy. "I Want a Wife." *Complements*. Ed. Anna Katsavos and Elizabeth Wheeler. New York: McGraw, 1994. 126–28.

Use a colon after the main title to introduce a subtitle.

> Haskell, Molly. *Holding My Own in No Man's Land: Women and Men and Film and Feminism*. New York: Oxford UP, 1997.

Put a period after the title. If the title ends with a question mark or exclamation point, you don't need a period.

> McAllister, Matthew. "Britpop Is Coming!" *Newsday* 7 Jan. 1996 sec. 2: 19, 23.

▣ PUBLISHING INFORMATION FOR BOOKS

City of Publication   If several cities are listed on the title page, list the first one. Give the Postal Service two-letter abbreviation for the state unless the city is generally known. Follow the city (and state if needed) by a colon, then one space.

> Benardete, Doris, ed. *Mark Twain: Wit and Wisecracks*. Mount Vernon, NY: Peter Pauper, 1961.

Publisher   Use the brief name of the publisher without labels such as Inc., and Co., or Publishers. Abbreviate University Press as UP without periods. Follow the name of the publisher with a comma.

> Flagg, Fannie. *Fried Green Tomatoes at the Whistle Stop Cafe*. New York: McGraw, 1988.

> Tsai, Henry. *The Chinese Experience*. Bloomington: Indiana UP, 1986.

> Zipes, Jack. *Breaking the Magic Spell: Radical Theories of Folk and Fairy Tales*. Austin: U of Texas P, 1979.

Date   Give the most recent date of revision or copyright as listed on the back of the title page. End each entry with a period.

> Walker, Alice. *Everything We Love Can Be Saved: A Writer's Activism.* New York: Random, 1997.

▣ PUBLISHING INFORMATION FOR PRINTED ARTICLES

Title of Magazine, Journal, or Newspaper   Underline or italicize the title of the work in which the article appeared, followed by a space and no punctuation.

> Ferris, Timothy. "The Year the Warning Lights Flashed On: Disasters of High Technology from the Past, Present and Maybe the Future." *Life* Jan. 1987: 67–71.

Volume Number   Do not give the volume or issue number for newspapers or popular magazines. *Do* give the volume number for scholarly journals.

> Crouse, James, and Dale Trusheim. "How Colleges Can Correctly Determine Selection Benefits from the SAT." *Harvard Education Review* 61 (May 1991): 125–47.

> Napier, Kristine, and Laura Goldstein. "Master the Slender Life." *Prevention* May 1997: 115–20.

Date of Publication   Give the date of the publication in the following order: day, month (abbreviated), and year, with no commas between them, but with a colon and one space after the year.

> Leder, Jane Mersky. "Adult Sibling Rivalry." *Psychology Today* Jan.–Feb. 1993: 56–58.

> Seligman, Daniel. "Liberal Poker." *Fortune* 6 May 1991: 115.

For a scholarly journal, put the date in parentheses after the volume number.

> Berry, Wendell. "The Body and the Machine." *Parabola* 15 (Fall 1990): 66–74.

Section of Newspaper   After the date of a newspaper, insert a comma and give the edition or section name or section number (in Arabic numerals), if any, abbreviating as ed. or sec., followed by a colon, plus one space. If the section is identified by a letter, do not use *sec*; simply put the letter before the page number.

> Bleyer, Bill. "Diver Finds Cleaner Water." *Newsday* 28 Aug. 1995, sec. News: A16.

> Fisher, Ian. "On the Web, Where Eros Wears Glasses." *New York Times* 13 Aug. 1997: B1.

Page Numbers   Give the pages covered by the article.

- Use a hyphen to indicate consecutive pages. List no more than the last two digits of the second number if the number will be clear:

    114–18   179–202

- Use a comma for two separate pages (23, 29).

- Use a plus sign (23+) for more than two noncontinuous pages.

> Trip, Gabriel. "Why Wed?" *New York Times* 15 Nov. 1987, sec. 6: 24+.

- If the article is a chapter or an essay in a book, give all the information for the book and add the page numbers the chapter covered:

> Fuchs, Victor. "Why Married Mothers Work." *Reading Critically, Writing Well.* 3rd ed. Rise B. Axelrod and Charles R. Cooper, eds. New York: St. Martin's, 1995. 316–20.

☐ ADDITIONAL INFORMATION FOR ELECTRONIC AND OTHER NONPRINT SOURCES

When you cite nonprint sources, give enough information that the reader of your paper could find the source. If your paper is emphasizing the work of an individual in a collaborative work, put that person's name first. Between the title and production company, you may give names of other individuals, using an abbreviation that indicates their role—adapt. (adapter), comp. (composer), cond. (conductor), narr. (narrator), perf. (performer), or writ. (writer).

Article in print but read on computer   Give the author, title of the article (in quotation marks), title of the entire work (underlined or italicized), and publishing information of the original in print. Give the title of the database (underlined or italicized). Indicate whether CD-ROM or Online (write Electronic if unsure), the vendor, and the date you viewed it.

> "Exercise, Massagelike Therapy Aid Carpal-Tunnel Syndrome." *Arizona Republic.* 28 Dec. 1997: A26. *News.* Electronic. Nexis. 12 June 1998.

Article on the Internet   Give the author or organization, the title (underlined or italicized), date of publication or last revision, the organization if different from the author, the date you viewed it, and the address of the Web site surrounded by angle brackets.

> Rogers, John G. *Endangered and Threatened Wildlife and Plants.* 16 Feb. 1996. The Federal Register. 18 April 1998 <http://www.fws.gov/r9endspp/96 cnorwt.html>.

Audiocassette, compact disc, or record   Give the artist, title (underlined or italicized), format if other than compact disc (Audiocassette, Audiotape—for reel-to-reel tape—or LP), production company, plus the date of the production.

> Buckley, Betty, perf. *The Mystery of Edwin Drood.* Compos. and writ. Rupert Holmes. Audiocassette. Polygram, 1986.

> R.E.M. *Automatic for the People.* Warner, 1992.

Computer program   Give the name of the writer if known, the title of the program (underlined or italicized), the medium (Diskette, CD-ROM, or Magnetic tape), number of the edition (abbreviated ed.) or the version (abbreviated Vers.), the city, the producer, and the date.

> *LabanWriter.* Diskette. Vers. 3.24. Columbus: Ohio State U, 1996.

Film   Give the title (underlined or italicized), then Dir. followed by the name of the director, the format if other than film (Videocassette or Videodisc), the production company for that particular format, plus the date of the original production.

> Dumont, Margaret, perf. *Duck Soup.* Dir. Leo McCarey. Perf. Groucho, Harpo, Chico, and Zeppo Marx. Videocassette. MCA, 1933.

> *Ran.* Dir. Akira Kurosawa. Videocassette. CBS/Fox, 1985.

Internet See above or page 146 for the format for other Internet sources.

Interview Give the name of the person interviewed and [optional] his or her title in brackets. If you conducted the interview, indicate whether it was a personal or telephone interview. Give the location and date of the interview. If the interview was conducted online or on radio or television, add the name of the interviewer and the broadcast information. Add the word Transcript followed by a period if that is how you got the information.

> Sherman, Max R. [Dean Emeritus, Lyndon Baines Johnson School for Public Affairs]. Personal Interview. Austin, TX. 12 Oct. 1997.

> Zipes, Jack [Professor of German, U of Minnesota]. Interview with Brian Lehrer. *On the Line* WNYC-AM, New York. 5 Aug. 1997.

Lecture or speech Give the name of the person. Give the title of the talk (or a description such as Class Lecture or Commencement Address), and the name of the event, class, or the sponsoring organization. Give the location and date.

> McAllister, Marie. "Images of Women in Film: Victim or Avenger?" Conf. on Women and Violence. Nassau Community College. Garden City, NY. I4 Nov. 1996.

Radio or television program Give the name of the person you quoted or paraphrased, the title of the program (underlined or italicized), the station or network, and the date of original broadcast.

> Reich, Robert B. *Marketplace*. Nat'l Public Radio. 25 Mar. 1998.

Work of Art Give the artist, the title of the work (underlined or italicized) and information on where you saw it.

> McKim, Mead and White. *Pennsylvania Station*. Photograph in Nathan Silver. *Lost New York*. New York: Schocken, 1971. 33–38.

> O'Keeffe, Georgia. *Black Iris 1926*. Metropolitan Museum, Alfred Stieglitz Collection, New York.

▢ UNUSUAL SOURCES

In general, it is better to give too much information about an unusual source (one not found readily in libraries) than to be cautious about format. Give enough data in brackets about the publisher (if known) so that the reader of your paper could find the source.

> Berger, Bruce. "Dancing with Time." *American Way* [American Airlines] 15 Feb. 1992, 40+.

> Jengo, Jay. "25 Years of Star Trek." *The Inside Collector* [Northport, NY] May 1992: 57–62.

▢ MISSING INFORMATION

Use the following abbreviations to denote missing information:

No date of publication given.	n.d.
no place of publication or no publisher	n.p.
no page numbers	n.pag.

> United States. Federal Trade Commission. *Building a Better Credit Record.* Washington: GPO, n.d.

When very little information is available about the document, indicate in brackets whatever details you can deduce, adding a question mark if this is an educated guess on your part. If they are numbered, give the number of pages to indicate the length of the source.

> Cultural Assistance Center [for the Commission for Cultural Affairs of the City of New York]. *A Guide to New York City Museums.* 1977. n.pag.

> *Little Italy: Souvenir Book.* [New York]: n.p. [1983?]. 32 pp.

◼ Checking the Works Cited Against the Parenthetical Citations

Remember to avoid these pitfalls:

- You cannot include a source in the list of Works Cited if you didn't refer to it in your paper. Delete from your list any source that you didn't actually use.

- List a source whether you used it extensively or just once—and whether you used quotations from it, or paraphrased it, or summarized it.

- The wording of your citations within the paper must match the listing in the Works Cited.

- You won't list a person who was quoted in someone else's book or article; the Works Cited will only list the author of the work you used.

- When giving the title of an anonymous article, both the parenthetical citation and the entry in the Works Cited should begin with the same word from the article's title; for similar titles, use more than one word in the parenthetical citation.

A student paper using the MLA format is in the Appendix of this book; its Work Cited page is on page 204.

CHAPTER 33

CHART OF SAMPLE ENTRIES FOR MLA WORKS CITED

(CHECK YOUR ENTRIES HERE)

In the following examples, titles have been underlined. It is also correct to use italics for titles in place of underlining, but you must be consistent.

Your Works Cited page will not follow the order of this chart. See the Appendix in this book, page 204, for a Works Cited page in the correct format.

Source	*Information Needed*
Article in a magazine	Author [last name, first name]. "Title of Article." <u>Title of Journal</u> or <u>Magazine</u> Date: pages covered.
Article in a newspaper	Author. "Title of Article." <u>Title of Newspaper</u> Date, sec. [for section, if numbered]: pages covered.
Article in a scholarly journal	Author. "Title of Article." <u>Title of Journal</u> Volume number (Date): pages covered.
Article with no author listed	"Title of Article." <u>Title of Newspaper or Magazine</u> Date, sec. [for section, if any]: pages covered.
Article on the Internet (see Internet)	
Book—one author	Author [last name, first name]. <u>Title of Book</u>. City of Publication: Publisher, latest date of copyright.
Book or article, same author as for entry above	---. [three hyphens and a period, no spaces in between] Alphabetize by title. [Give all information as for any other work, even if there is repetition.]
Book—two authors	First Author [last name, first name], Second Author [first name first]. <u>Title of Book</u>. City of Publication: Publisher, latest date of copyright.

Sample Entries

Laboda, Amy. "The Organized Cockpit." Private Pilot

    Nov. 1993:34.

Dorman, Michael. "Who Killed Medgar Evers?" New York

    Times 17 May 1992, sec. 6:52+.

Shorris, Earl. "The Triumphant Power of the Humanities."

    American Educator 21 (Winter 1997-98):2-7+.

"Aldo Rossi 1931-1997." Architecture Oct. 1997: 27.

Heilbrun, Carolyn. The Education of a Woman. New York:

    Dell, 1995.

---. Writing a Woman's Life. New York: Ballantine, 1988.

Dingus, Lowell, and Timothy Rowe. The Mistaken

    Extinction: Dinosaur Evolution and the Origin of

    Birds. New York: Freeman, 1998.

Source	*Information Needed*
Book—three authors	First Author [last name, first name], Second Author [first name first], Third Author [first name first]. <u>Title of Book</u>. City of Publication: Publisher, latest date of copyright.
Book—more than three authors or editors	First Author or Editor listed on title page [last name, first name], et al. [for "and others"]. <u>Title of Book</u>. City of Publication: Publisher, latest date of copyright.
Book, not first edition	Author or Editor, ed. [for editor if necessary]. <u>Title of Book</u>. Number of edition [written in digit plus suffix]. City of Publication: Publisher, latest date of copyright.
Book with editor (no author listed)	Editor [last name, first name], ed. [for editor]. <u>Title of Book</u>. City of Publication: Publisher, latest date of copyright.
Book with both editor and author	Author [last name, first name]. <u>Title of Book</u>. Ed. [for editor] Editor's name [first name first]. City of Publication: Publisher, latest date of copyright.
Book by an organization	Name of Organization in normal order. <u>Title of Book</u>. City of Publication: Publisher [even if it is the same as the organization], latest date of copyright.

Sample Entries

Jaffe, Jerome, Robert Petersen, and Ray Hodgson.

　　Addictions: Issues and Answers. New York: Harper,

　　1980.

Duquette, Donald N., et al. Advocating for the Child in

　　Protection Proceedings: A Handbook for Lawyers and

　　Court-Appointed Special Advocates. Lexington, MA:

　　Lexington, 1990.

Perrine, Laurence. Sound and Sense: An Introduction to

　　Poetry. 6th ed. San Diego: Harcourt, 1993.

Oldman, Mark, and Samer Hamadeh, eds. America's Top

　　Internships, 1999. Princeton: Princeton Review,

　　1998.

Bulfinch, Thomas. The Art of Fable, or Beauties of

　　Mythology. Ed. William H. Klapp. New York: Tudor,

　　1935.

United States. Federal Trade Commission. Building a

　　Better Credit Record. Washington: GPO, n.d.

Source	*Information Needed*
Book review (use this form also for film and theater reviews)	Reviewer's name [last name, first name]. "Title of the Review." Rev. [for "review"] of <u>Title of the Work Reviewed,</u> by Name of Author or Artist [first name first]. <u>Title of Magazine or Newspaper</u> Date: pages covered.
Chapter or essay in edited book	Author of Chapter or Essay [last name, first name]. "Title of Chapter." <u>Title of Book</u>. Ed. [for editor] Name of Editor [first name first]. City of Publication: Publisher, latest copyright date. numbers of the pages covered.
Computer program	Author (if known). <u>Title</u>. CD-ROM [or Diskette or Magnetic tape]. City: Production Company, date.
Database	Author [if given]. "Title of Article." Date. <u>Title of Database</u>. CD-ROM or Online [or Electronic if unsure] Name of Computer Service. Date viewed.
Editorial or op-ed piece	Author if given. "Title." Editorial [or Op-ed]. <u>Title of Periodical</u>. Date: page.
Encyclopedia article	"Title of Article." <u>Title of Encyclopedia</u>. Number of edition [digit plus suffix]. CD-ROM [if applicable].

Sample Entries

Rubin, Hanna. "The City's Front Yard." Rev. of A Year in

Central Park, by Laurie A. Walters. New York Times

25 Oct. 1992, sec. 7:20.

Atwood, Margaret. "Homelanding." A Writer's Reader.

Ed. Donald Hall and D. L. Emblem. 8th ed. New York:

HarperCollins, 1997. 32-34.

Cinemania 97. CD-ROM. Redmond: Microsoft, 1996.

"Apple Helps Batman and Robin Take Flight." 24 June

1997. Presswire. Electronic. Nexis. 23 July 1997.

Sava, Samuel G. "Maybe Computers Aren't Schools'

Salvation." Op-ed. New York Times 6 Sept. 1997: 14.

"Biblical Literature and Its Critical Interpretation."

Encyclopaedia Britannica: Macropaedia. 15th ed.

Source	*Information Needed*
Film	Title of film. Dir. Name of director [first name first]. Format if other than film. Production company for the format, date of original production. Optional: running time in minutes.
Film review (see book review)	
Government publication	Name of Government. Author or Agency. Title of Publication. City: Publisher [use GPO for Government Printing Office], date.
Illustration, cartoon, or photograph, independent of surrounding text	Artist if given. "Title" if given. Drawing [or Cartoon or Photograph]. Title of Periodical. Date: page.
Illustration, painting, or other work of art	Artist. Title of Illustration. Date created, if given. Where you viewed it.
Illustration, photograph, or graphic accompanying text	Artist. "Title [if given]." [If no title, give a brief description]. In Author. [Give complete title and other information for source.]

Sample Entries

Rambling Rose. Dir. Martha Coolidge. Laserdisc. LIV.

    1991. 140 min.

United States. National Governors' Association. Results

    in Education: State-Level College Assessment

    Initiatives—1987–88: Results of a Fifty-State

    Survey. Washington: GPO, 1985.

Lorenz, Lee. Cartoon. New Yorker 20 Mar. 1995: 61.

O'Keefe, Georgia. Black Abstraction 1927. Georgia

    O'Keefe. New York: Viking, 1976. Plate 54.

Picasso, Pablo. Les Demoiselles d'Avignon. 1907. Museum

    of Mod. Art, New York. 1997. 15 May 1999

    <http://www.moma.org/collection/

    paintsculpt/picasso.demoiselles.html>.

Leachman, Jim. Photographs. In R. Craig Kirkpatrick.

    "Search for the Snub-Nosed Monkey." Natural History

    Apr. 1997: 42–47.

Source	*Information Needed*
Internet article	Author or organization [if known]. "Title of the Article." <u>Title of the Web site</u> [if given]. Date of publication or last revision [if given]. Sponsoring organization if given and different from author. Date you viewed it <Internet address of the site>.
Internet message (personal e-mail)	Author [title or area of expertise]. E-mail to the author [meaning you]. Date.
Internet posting (message to a Usenet news group)	Real name of author. "The subject line of the article." Online posting. The date of the posting. The group to which it was sent—multiple groups separated by a comma. Date you viewed it <where the article can be retrieved>.
Interview	Name of Interviewee [Interviewee's Job Title]. Personal [or telephone] interview. City. Date.
Introduction, foreword, preface, or afterword to a book	Author. Introduction [or other label]. Title of Book. By Author of Book. City: Publisher: date. Pages covered.

Sample Entries

Still, Keith. "Mind the Gaps." Last Word Archive. 1997.

New Scientist. 16 May 1999

<http://www.last-word.com/lastword/answers/

lwa649mysteries.html>.

Young, Sally, Ph.D. [Director of Freshman Writing

Program, U of Tennessee]. E-mail to the author.

13 Dec. 1997.

Little, Gordon S. "Re: Creating the Gender." Online

posting. 9 Aug. 1997. <soc.men, alt.men's-rights,

alt.politics.correct> 9 Sept. 1997

<http://xp7.dejanews.com/getdoc.xp7>.

Sherman, Max [Dean, Lyndon Baines Johnson School of

Public Affairs]. Personal Interview. Austin, TX.

21 May 1997.

Davis, Thadious M. Introduction. Plays by Aishah Rahman.

By Aishah Rahman. New York: Broadway Play:

1997. v-ix.

Source	*Information Needed*
Lecture or speech	Name of Presenter. "Title of Presentation" [or course]. Location. Date.
Letter to the editor	Author of letter. "Title [if given]." Title of Periodical date: page.
Newspaper (see article in a newspaper)	
Pamphlet	Author or organization. Title. City of publication: publisher, date. Indicate missing information–n.p. (no publisher) or n.d. (no date) or give your best guess in brackets.
Radio or television program	Presenter(s) of the Information. Title of Program. Network [if any]. Call Letters of Broadcasting Station [plus AM, FM, or TV]. Date of broadcast.
Videocassette, film, audiotape, or CD.	Artist or Author. Title. Videocassette [or other format]. Producer or Company, date. Running time or engineering specifics.
Visit to a site	Name of site. City, two-letter designation for state (if necessary). Date of visit.
Web site (see Internet article)	

Sample Entries

McAllister, Marie. "Images of Women in Film: Victim

or Avenger?" Conf. on Women and Violence. Nassau

Community College. Garden City, NY. 14 Nov. 1996.

Gazzarniga, Marin. Letter. "Until Working Father Joins

Superwoman." New York Times 31 Mar. 1991: E2.

John, Nicholas. "Fatal Attractions: Carmen and Her

Admirers." Carmen Jones. [Playbill at the Old Vic

Theatre]. London: 1991. n.pag.

Moyers, Bill, and Robert Bly. A Gathering of Men. PBS.

WNET TV. 8 Jan. 1990.

Rosen, Peter, dir. First Person Singular: I. M. Pei.

Videocassette. PBS Fox, 1997. 90 min.

Corning Glass Works. Ithaca, NY. 2 Oct. 1997.

CHAPTER 34

THE APA STYLE
(SOCIAL AND NATURAL SCIENCES)

The APA (American Psychological Association) style for reporting research is similar to the MLA style, except it emphasizes the date of publication, both in the parenthetical citations and in the list of references at the end. Use this system for papers in the natural sciences or the social sciences (for example, economics, psychology, and sociology). For history and political science, you may need to use footnotes (see Chapter 35).

▪ CITATIONS

With this method, both the name of the author and the date are given in the paper whenever information is presented. Here are the most common forms:

> Keen (1991) described how masculinity and aggression are intertwined in American social values.

> The way our society treats girls and boys while they are growing up explains the problems that women and men have in communication (Tannen 1986).

The preferred way is to use the author's last name in your sentence:

> Tannen (1990) contrasted the American cultural rearing of girls and boys.

Note that in APA style, the author's work is described in the past tense ("contrasted").

For a direct quotation—but not for a paraphrase—the page number is also given, with the abbreviation p. or pp.

Here is a paragraph using the APA style:

Keen (1991) described how boys are taught assertiveness (even aggression) at a very young age to prove their masculinity. Girls, however, are brought up to control their aggressive feelings, and to prove their femininity by caring about others. Besides being governed by different codes of behavior, according to Tannen (1990), the sexes "grow up in different worlds of words" (p. 43). The way our society treats girls and boys while they are growing up explains the problems that women and men have in communication (Tannen 1986). These labels of what is "masculine" or what is "feminine" deny the fact that all human beings have a range of feelings—sometimes needing to connect with others and at other times needing to be independent or dominant. As Steinem (1992) observed:

> The little boy who is ridiculed for crying "like a girl" doesn't stop feeling sad, he just buries that emotion; and the little girl who is punished for willfulness as a "tomboy" just takes that spirit underground. (p. 257)

Notice how these citations have been used; they represent the most common forms:

- The first citation includes only the date; the name of the author has already been given, and this is a paraphrase so you don't need a page number.

- The second citation gives the date after the author's name, indicating which work is cited.

- The third citation is after a direct quotation of a phrase. Since the author and date have already been given, only the page number is necessary.

- The fourth citation requires the author's name because it has not been given in the sentence. No page number is given, because this is not a direct quotation. The date, 1986, tells you that this is a different book by Tannen.

- The fifth citation gives the date of Steinem's book.

- The last citation is after a direct quotation. The author's name introduced the quotation, so only the page number is needed. This quotation is set off because it's longer than three lines.

■ SPECIAL CASES

- Information from sources that cannot be consulted by your reader (lectures, interviews, personal letters, phone conversations, or E-mail messages) should be identified as such, with the date in parentheses. Do not include the source in your reference list.

> In an interview, Dr. Thorpy (November 6, 1997) said that "the only people who can change this problem are the ones who are having trouble sleeping."

- For **two authors,** join the last names with *and* if the reference is in your sentence or with an ampersand (&) when using parentheses.

> Halpern and Coren (1991) found a connection between right-handedness and longevity.

> Left-handed individuals did not live as long as the right-handed people in the study (Halpern & Coren 1991).

- For **three to six authors,** give all the names for the first reference. Thereafter, use only the last name of the first author plus *et al.* (meaning "and others").

> Feenberg, Mitrusi, & Poterba (1997) analyzed retail purchases of food and clothing as a percentage of income.

> A national retail sales tax would impose more of a hardship on low-income families (Feenberg et al. 1997).

- For **more than six authors,** give only the last name of the first author plus *et al.*—whether in your sentence or in parentheses.

> Petrill et al. (1996) identified DNA markers for certain cognitive abilities.

> DNA markers have been identified for certain cognitive abilities (Petrill et al. 1996).

▣ REFERENCES

The APA style follows all the rules that we have already given for the Works Cited page according to the MLA system (see the previous chapter for individual cases), with these exceptions:

- The list is called *References*, and the first line of each entry is indented five spaces.

- Give only the initials for the first and middle names of authors, and give all names in reverse order—even for multiple authors. List all authors up to six (and then use et al.).

> Page, L., Burr, B. (1991). <u>Peterson's field guide to freshwater fishes: North America, north of Mexico.</u> New York: Houghton Mifflin.

> Petrill, S.A., et al. (1996). DNA markers associated with general and specific cognitive abilities. <u>Intelligence, 23,</u> 191–203.

- For authors who have written more than one work, repeat the name for each entry.

> Lubinski, D., & Benbow, C. P (1992). Gender differences in abilities and preferences among the gifted: Implications for the math/science pipeline. <u>Current Directions in Psychological Science 1,</u> 61–66.

> Lubinski, D., & Benbow, C. P. (1995). An opportunity for empiricism: Review of Howard Gardner's <u>Multiple intelligences: the theory in practice.</u> <u>Contemporary Psychology.</u> <u>40,</u> 935–938.

- The year for each entry is placed within parentheses—right after the author's or editor's name:

> Benbow, C. P., & Lubinski, D. (Eds.) (1996). <u>Intellectual talent: Psychometric and social issues.</u> Baltimore: Johns Hopkins University Press.

- When listing an author with two or more works with the same date, list the works alphabetically and distinguish among the works by adding a letter to the date—for example, 1995a, 1995b, 1995c.

> Halpern, D. F. (1996a). Changing data, changing minds: What the data on cognitive sex differences tell us and what we hear. <u>Learning and Individual Differences, 8,</u> 71–80.

> Halpern, D.F. (1996b). <u>Thinking critically about critical thinking</u>. Rahweh, NJ: Erlbaum.

- For articles, give the month and day (if given) in the parentheses after the year. Place a comma after the year and do not abbreviate the month.

> Hill, C. E., Diemer, R. A., & Heaton, K. J. (1997, January). Dream interpretation sessions: Who volunteers, who benefits, and what volunteer clients view as most and least helpful. <u>Journal of Counseling Psychology</u>, <u>44</u>, 53–62.

- Capitalize only the first word of titles and subtitles, and any proper names, for books, encyclopedias, and articles, but capitalize all main words of titles of newspapers, magazines, and scholarly journals.

> Curiosity killed the bat. (1989, November). <u>Natural History</u>, p. 62.

- Underline (do not italicize) the titles of books, newspapers, and magazines, but do not use quotation marks around the titles of articles, essays, and chapters.

> Dorman, M. (1992, May 17). Who killed Medgar Evers? <u>New York Times</u>, sec. 6, pp. 52+.

- Use p. or pp. to indicate the page number(s) for articles in magazines and newspapers or for chapters in books.

> Stevenson, J. (1992, September 21). Food for naught. <u>New Republic</u>, pp. 13–14, 16.

- For scholarly journals, give the volume number underlined, followed by a comma and then the page number(s). Do not use vol., or p. or pp. Give all digits for page numbers.

> Kenny, M. E., & Rice, K. G. (1995). Attachment to parents in late adolescent college students: Current status, applications, and future considerations. <u>The Counseling Psychologist</u>, <u>23</u>, 433–456.

- Use p. or pp. to indicate the page number(s) for articles in magazines and newspapers, or for chapters in books.

> Stevenson, J. (1992, September 21). Food for naught. <u>New Republic</u>, pp. 13–14, 16.

- Do not abbreviate publishers' names; do abbreviate *and* with &. Do not include "Co.," "Inc.," or "Publisher." Do include "University" and "Press."

  Burka, J. B., & Yuen, L. (1983). Procrastination: Why you do it, what to do about it. Toronto: Addison Wesley.

  Furstenberg, F. F., & Harris, K. M. (1993). When and why fathers matter: Impacts of father involvement on the children of adolescent mothers. In R. I. Lerman & T. J. Ooms (Eds.). Young unwed fathers: Changing roles and emerging policies (pp. 117–138). Philadelphia: Temple University Press.

- List a Web site or electronically retrieved article just as you would if it were in print. Then give the appropriate electronic information and the date you viewed it if relevant. Use *n.d.* ["no date"] if the date is not given. Do not place a period after the Internet address.

  Amato, P. R. (1992, December). Contact with non-custodial fathers and children's wellbeing. Family Matters, 36, pp. 32–34. Retrieved November 6, 1997 from the World Wide Web: http://www.1.tpgi.com.au/users/resolve/ncreeport/amato (1993).html

  The Nature Conservancy. (n.d.). Dolan falls preserve. Retrieved March 4, 1998 from the World Wide Web: http://www.tnc.org/infield/preserve/dolan

  Yevoli, Carole. (1993). Corrective strategies in reading for at-risk community college students. ERIC ED366370. Retrieved online November 7, 1997. http://eric.syr.edu

- Do not list sources for any communication that could not be studied by your reader—for example, interviews, E-mail messages, and lectures. Refer to the source of the information in the body of your paper, mentioning the type of communication. Do not include the source in your reference list.

For a complete paper using APA Style, see the Appendix in this book, pages 205–215.

CHAPTER 35

THREE OTHER STYLES

(THE ACS STYLE, FOOTNOTES, AND ENDNOTES)

This chapter explains three other systems of documentation. Particular academic disciplines use variations of these formats. Ask your instructor which style to use.

- For physical sciences: The ACS System

- The classic style: footnotes and bibliography (used in communications, history, and political science)

- A variation: endnotes

All three of these systems give a number in the text that then matches the full reference, similarly numbered at the foot of each page or at the end of the paper.

▨ FOR PHYSICAL SCIENCES: THE ACS SYSTEM

The American Chemical Society (ACS) system is used in mathematics, chemistry, and physics.

CITATIONS

- Each reference is given a number in the order of appearance in the paper. These numbers match the list of numbered references at the end of the paper.

- The number for the source is repeated in the text every time that source is credited for information.

- In the text, the numbers are raised and placed right after the information.

  A good presentation of how these principles operate in computer-assisted design is Leendert Ammeraal's description of "finite solid objects that are essentially bounded flat faces."[8]

- Multiple numbers indicate that the respectively numbered sources agree or have data on that point. Use a comma (,) to mean *and*, and use a hyphen (-) to mean *through*.

  There are also options that allow you to make an image look as if wind were blowing it away or as if it were made up of tiles.[2-5]

REFERENCES

For every entry **list sources** (and number them only once) in the order in which they are referred to in the paper rather than in alphabetical order as with other systems. Thus, number one is the source mentioned first in the paper, no matter how often it is again referred to; number four is the fourth new reference in the paper.

- Start the list on a new page. Center and boldface the title, References (without quotation marks or underline).

- Single-space the list, but skip a line between entries.

- Begin at the left margin with the number for each entry enclosed in parentheses, without a period.

- Indent two spaces after the number for every line.

- End each entry with a period.

  (1) Ferris, T. *Life* **1987** 10 (1), 67–7.

Authors

- Reverse all the authors' names and give only initials for first and middle names; use semicolons between the names. List all multiple authors.

  (2) Jaschek, C.; Jaschek, M. <u>The Classification of the Stars</u>; Cambridge: New York, 1987.

Books

- Italicize the titles of books, followed by a semicolon.

- Give the name of the publisher, followed by a colon and two spaces, then the city of publication followed by a comma and one space, and the date.

> (3) Suffness, M. *Taxol: Science and Applications;* CRC Press: New York, 1995.

Articles

- Do not give the title of the article for journal articles.

- Abbreviate and italicize the title of the journal, followed by the year (boldfaced or underlined with a wavy line but without punctuation), followed by a space, and then the volume number, no space, the issue number in parentheses, a comma, no space, and then the page numbers.

> (4) Hsu, J. R; Schattenberg, H. J., 111; Garza, M. M. *J. Assoc. of Anal. Chem.* 1991 74(5), 886–892.

Here is a paragraph by Eric Jergenson, a student, using ACS citations, followed by the *References* page for his entire paper.

> In 1837, Dr. C. G. Page of Salem, Massachusetts, was experimenting with a primitive battery, a coil, and some horseshoe magnets.[1–2] He knew that the wet-cell battery, invented by Volta in 1800,[3] stored an electrical charge and was capable of furnishing an electric current. Page also knew that electric currents flow due to voltage, which is an electrical pressure, through an electrical circuit.[2-3] What Page was not aware of was the properties of coils or the concept of induction, the process by which a body with electrical or magnetic properties creates similar properties in a neighboring body without direct contact.[2-3] When the coil was attached to the battery and one or both poles of the magnet were placed by the coil, a ringing sound was heard in the magnet when connections to the battery were either made or broken. Page believed that the sound was the reverberation of the snapping sound made when connections to the battery were made or broken.[1] Actually, the coil became magnetized by the flow of current from

the battery and through electromagnetic induction, the magnets were caused to vibrate whenever the circuit was made or broken.[2-3]

Note: Normally, references are on a separate page.

References

(1) Eiche, J. E. *What's a Synthesizer: Simple Answers to Common Questions about the Musical Technology;* Leonard Books: Milwaukee, 1987.

(2) Schrader, B. *Introduction to Electro-Acoustic Music;* Prentice Hall: Englewood Cliffs, NJ, 1982.

(3) Horn, D. T. *Digital Electronic Music Synthesizers;* Tab Books: Blue Ridge Summit, PA, 1988.

(4) Charbeneau, T. *Futurist.* **1987** 21(5), 35–7.

(5) Mathews, M. V.; Pierce, J. R. *Sci. Amer.* **1987** 256(2), 126–33.

(6) Thompson, T. *Bus. Wk.* **1987** (40), 114–16.

☐ THE CLASSIC STYLE: FOOTNOTES AND BIBLIOGRAPHY

This traditional system is the best choice for a report for a general audience or for courses in art, communications, dance, journalism, music, theater, history, or political science.

With footnotes, you place a raised numeral in your paper every time you present information from your research—either at the end of the summary, paraphrase, or quotation (after the quotation marks), or within the sentence, right after the fact or statistic. The raised numeral is then repeated at the bottom of that page (see the example below), with the specific source of the information. The MLA formerly used this system, and they still explain how to do it.[1]

---

[1] Joseph Gibaldi, <u>MLA Handbook for Writers of Research Papers</u> 4th ed. (New York: MLA, 1995), 242–56.

The numbers for this footnoting system are continuous; that is, you begin with the number one and progress, using the next number each time you document a fact or quotation from your research. Thus, one source may be referred to several times, but each new use of material from that source will have a new number. After the first complete footnote, subsequent footnotes for that source give only the last name of the author and the appropriate page number.[2]

The advantages of this system are that if readers are curious about the source, they can easily glance down to the bottom of the page. The writer of the paper can make interpretive or explanatory comments.[3]

The disadvantage is that you have to plan carefully so that the number in the text and the correspondingly numbered footnote are on the same page. Computers, however, simplify this task.

FORMAT FOR FOOTNOTES

- Footnotes begin at the bottom of the page—four lines below the last line of text—and correspond to the numbers given in the text on that page.

- First draw a two-inch line (twelve strokes of the underline key) and skip a line.

- Indent five spaces and give the appropriate raised numeral.

- Skip a space and give the name of the author, first name first.

- Follow the author's name with a comma and a space.

For Books

- Give the title, underlined, followed by a space. Give the name of an editor or a number for the edition, if necessary, after a comma; otherwise use no punctuation.

- After an opening parenthesis, give first the city of publication, followed by a colon and one space.

---

[2] Gibaldi, 3.
[3] The footnote can add a comment that would otherwise clutter up your paper.

- Then give the name of the publisher, followed by a comma and one space.

- Give the date of copyright, then a closing parenthesis, followed by a comma, then a space.

- Give the page number(s), without p. or pp.

- End the entry with a period.

⁴ Joseph Gibaldi, MLA Handbook for Writers of Research Papers, 4th ed. (New York: MLA, 1995), 183–200.

For Articles

- Give the title of the article in quotation marks, with a comma inside the closing quotation marks.

- After one space, give the title of the periodical, underlined and followed by no punctuation.

- Give the volume number for scholarly journals and enclose the date in parentheses, followed by a comma.

⁵ Lynn Veach Sadler, "Spinsters, Non-Spinsters, and Men in the World of Barbara Pym." Critique 30 (Spring 1985), 141–154.

- Give the date of a nonscholarly periodical—day, month, and year with no punctuation and one space between—followed by a colon and two spaces.

⁶ Peter Schrag, "The Near Myth of Our Failing Schools." Atlantic Monthly Oct. 1997: 72.

- Give the page number(s) followed by a period.

You may use *Ibid.* [meaning "the same"] plus the page number in a footnote for the same reference as the one directly preceding it. However, it is also correct, and easier, to give only the author's last name and the specific page number for subsequent citations.

Here is an example of a paragraph using footnotes. Check the numerals and the matching footnotes at the bottom of the page:

> Frank Campion analyzes how health insurance changed the way Americans pay doctors and hospitals. After the institution of

Medicaid and Medicare, medical costs "rose rapidly."[7] At the same time, insurance "substantially reduced and in some cases eliminated out of pocket cost for all but 10–15 percent of the population."[8]

FORMAT FOR BIBLIOGRAPHY

The *Bibliography*, at the end of the paper, is a list of all the sources referred to in the footnotes. Each source is listed only once, in alphabetical order by the authors' last names (not in the order you used them), and in the same format as for the Works Cited page, described in Chapter 32, "Works Cited," and Chapter 33, "Chart of Sample Entries."

In addition, this system allows you to list a *Supplementary Bibliography*, a list of sources that you read for background or tangential information but did not actually use to write the report.

☐ A Variation: Endnotes

This system is the same as the footnote system, except the footnotes are moved from the foot of each page and are instead accumulated in numerical order at the end of the paper on a separate page, called *Notes*. This method simplifies the typing, but it has a disadvantage for the reader who must leaf back and forth to check the sources.

FORMAT FOR ENDNOTES

- After the title, *Notes* (centered), skip two lines and indent the first line five spaces.

- Give the raised numeral, skip a space, and then begin the note.

- Use the same format as for footnotes (see page 160).

- Double-space the entire page.

Use the same format for the Bibliography as described in Chapter 32, "Works Cited," and Chapter 33, "Chart of Sample Entries."

---

[7] Frank Campion The AMA and J.S Health Policy since 1940 (Chicago: Chicago Review, 1984), 507.
[8] Ibid. 506.

CHAPTER 36

IN A CRUNCH 5
(KEEP THE SPIRIT OF THE LAW)

☐ YOUR PAPER HAS TO BE DOCUMENTED—NO MATTER WHAT

The purpose of documentation is to tell where you found each piece of information in a way that your reader could then go and find it—to the exact page.

If you're unsure about the details of your documentation, include this information as closely as possible to the required form as shown in Chapters 31, 32, and 33. Then explain to your teacher, either in writing or face to face, what your problems are.

☐ MARK CITATIONS IN YOUR ROUGH DRAFT WITH A HIGHLIGHTER

Once the citations are highlighted, you can see more easily any punctuation and spelling errors. Most citations will include an author's last name and a page number, without punctuation: (Smith 182).

☐ CHECK FOR PLAGIARISM

Read your paper aloud. If a passage is hard to read, it probably is not your wording. Be vigilant in checking against the sources you have used, particularly if you downloaded material.

Remember that you must give credit (with a parenthetical citation) for the ideas and facts you used, even if you did rephrase them, and that the words of others must be quoted correctly.

☐ ALPHABETIZE YOUR WORKS CITED ON A COMPUTER

If you can, use a computer to arrange your Works Cited alphabetically. If you have to manually alphabetize your sources, put each on a separate notecard and alphabetize before you begin to type. After typing, check to be sure that the second line of each entry is indented five spaces and that you have a period at the end of each entry.

☐ CHECK YOUR WORKS CITED PAGE AGAINST YOUR CITATIONS

Make a final check to ensure that you have not either left out a source on your Works Cited page or added a source that you didn't end up using. Remember, no source should be listed in your Works Cited page if you didn't actually use information from it.

Note: These suggestions use the details of documentation for the MLA style. If you need to follow one of the styles listed in Chapters 34 or 35, check there for the fine points.

PART 6

FINISHING YOUR PAPER

CHAPTER 37

LARGE-SCALE REVISION
(THE BIG PICTURE)

There are two kinds of revision: *large-scale* and *small-scale*. First you need to look at the overall content of your paper. Later you will concern yourself with the details. It's foolish at this stage to fine-tune details that eventually might get cut out of your paper.

◼ MAKE A QUICK LIST OF THE MAIN IDEAS IN YOUR PAPER

A good way to see your paper as a whole is to write an outline of the actual paper that you have written. Write down a main phrase from each paragraph in the paper.

◼ ORGANIZATION

Now study the sequence of ideas in your list of phrases.

- Are related points together?

- Is the sequence logical?

- Is the same point or quotation repeated in different parts of your paper?

Still working with your list, rearrange or cut any points that seem repetitious or out of place. Then make the corresponding changes in your paper.

This method also helps your paragraphing:

- Divide a paragraph that has two main points.

- Delete a paragraph that repeats a point.

- Expand a paragraph that is underdeveloped; add information or explanation.

☐ Emphasis

Make sure your thesis, or major point, is clear early in the paper.

Have you featured the most important facts?   Be careful not to bury the most significant point in the middle of a paragraph or series. The middle is the weakest position in any list; the final position is the strongest.

Be ruthless.   Don't include a fact or opinion or quotation or joke just because you like it. One of the most painful parts of the writing process is to *let go*—to admit that an interesting fact just does not contribute to the point you are stressing and will divert the reader from that point.

☐ Completeness

Check your list of main points for gaps in logic or information. Where they are needed, add appropriate details.

If you wrote an outline when you were planning your paper, check that original outline against the list you have just written and reorganize or fill in gaps as necessary.

☐ Evidence

Make sure that you have sufficient evidence and explanation. A strong research paper will back up every general assertion with facts, examples, or logical reasons.

You may find that you do not have sufficient evidence for a point; if so, you will need to go back and do a little more research.

☐ Clarity

Will your reader be able to follow your line of thought and understand each individual point?

• **Terms** You might need to explain or define some terms.

- **Quotations** The reader needs to know who said them and how each one fits the point you are making.

- **Facts** Make clear how each fact fits in with what you are saying.

- **Complex concepts** Have you taken the reader with you step by step?

◼ INTRODUCTION AND CONCLUSION

Now is the time to take a second look at your introduction and conclusion. Think about what your paper says, and make sure the introduction points the way. Your conclusion should do more than just repeat your main points: It should leave the reader with a final emphasis, the point you most want to stress.

Write both the introduction and conclusion with energy and force. If you get stumped in coming up with an intriguing introduction or conclusion, study a few good magazines or newspaper articles to give you some ideas. Then draft out a few alternatives to see which ones feel right. You don't want to slide into your paper at the start or to limp out of it at the end.

◼ TITLE

Check that your preliminary title still fits the main idea of your paper. It should point to the specific aspect of the topic on which you are concentrating.

One option is to give your paper two titles. It is common to do so, putting a colon between them. One half can be poetic, the other half can be informative.

> Killing Dolphins: As Easy as Opening a Can of Tuna

> The Voice of the Land: The Prairie in Willa Cather's <u>My Antonia</u>

Remember not to use quotation marks or underlining for your own title.

CHAPTER 38

SMALL–SCALE REVISION
(DETAILS THAT COUNT)

Small-scale revision means looking closely at the details of your paper so that your reader won't get distracted by your mistakes.

☐ ACCURACY

Numbers and names   Make sure that they are correctly copied.

Quotations   Make sure every quotation is a word-for-word reproduction of the original and that you have quotation marks around all wording taken directly from your sources.

Documentation   Remember that whether the information from a source is in your words (needing no quotation marks) or someone else's (and therefore framed by quotation marks), you must have a citation identifying its source.

Citations of sources   Make sure that the author and page number are accurate for all citations. Use a highlighter pen to mark citations in your rough draft so that they stand out from the rest of the paper. That way you can more easily see and correct them.

☐ STYLE

Make sure you have put information into your own style of writing rather than heavily quoting or merely changing a few words from your sources. An essential step in checking the style of your paper is to read it out loud. As you read aloud, listen for places that seem too wordy, too formal, or too informal.

- **Be clear**. Use plain English as much as possible instead of technical jargon. You don't want to pad your paper with wordy phrases, such as "due to the fact that."

- **Don't be too informal**. Avoid slang, cliches, and cute little remarks to the reader ("Ha! Ha!"). Do not refer to authors on a first-name basis ("Ben says . . . ").

- **Omit "I think" phrases**. It is unnecessary to apologize for your own opinion with phrases such as "I think" or "in my opinion." Your teacher knows who is expressing these ideas.

- **Strengthen weak phrasing.** Use active verbs (*reported* or *stated*) rather than passive verbs ("It was stated"). Delete meaningless modifiers (*nice, interesting, weird*).

▣ TRANSITIONS

The flow of your paper depends on your providing a smooth transition from one sentence to the next, from one paragraph to the next, and from one idea to the next. Check to see if your paper moves smoothly from one part to the other. If not, go back and add transitional words and phrases that will show the relationship between your sentences, paragraphs, and ideas.

For example, at the beginning of each paragraph, make clear how it builds on the previous paragraph and how the two major ideas are connected. Here are a few commonly used transitions:

However	Nevertheless	For example
On the other hand	In any case	Despite the evidence
Therefore	Furthermore	In addition to

Directive expressions.   A special type of transition particular to research papers—*directive expressions*—links your ideas to the quotations and facts from your sources. Here are some directive expressions that you might find useful:

According to Loren Eiseley . . .	Bettelheim points out that . . .
Bulfinch maintains that . . .	Adrienne Rich says . . .
In Atwood's opinion . . .	Bill Moyers argues that . . .

■ Grammar and Usage

This is the point at which to check and double-check punctuation, spelling, and any aspect of grammar and usage that gives you trouble. Use a dictionary and a handbook such as *Rules of Thumb: A Guide for Writers*.

Check for the following:

- **Spelling**   Use the spellcheck (and grammar check if your computer has one).

- **Confusing words**   Check the spelling of words that are often confused such as *to* and *too*, *then* and *than*. A computer spellcheck will miss this type of error.

- **Complete sentences**   Look at the placement of periods to avoid run-on sentences and sentence fragments. Particularly check where you have incorporated quotations into your own sentences.

- **Verb tenses**   Make sure you have not shifted back and forth between present and past tenses.

- **Punctuation**   Check especially that commas and other punctuation used with quotations are correct. Remember that commas and periods go *inside* quotation marks except when a parenthetical citation follows the quotation.

- **Titles**   Check that titles of books, periodicals, and other long works are underlined or italicized and that titles of articles, chapters, and other short works are enclosed in quotation marks.

■ Documentation

Check to be sure that:

All information is credited.   This includes not only direct quotations but paraphrases and summaries.

Page numbers of all citations are accurate.   Be sure each citation from a printed source has a page number and that the number is accurate.

Punctuation is correct around citations.   Check commas, semicolons, and periods around parentheses and quotation marks; be certain each parenthesis and each quotation mark has a partner. Remember that in the most common citation—author's last name and page number—you do not use any punctuation (no comma or p.).

The Works Cited is complete.   Make sure that you have listed in your Works Cited each source that you have referred to in your paper. Also, be sure that you do not include in the Works Cited any source that you did not take material directly from, even though you may have read that source.

The parenthetical citations match those listed in the Works Cited. Check each parenthetical citation to be certain that it corresponds exactly with the first word of the corresponding entry in your Works Cited.

Each Works Cited entry ends with a period.   Check to be sure that you have put a period at the end of each Works Cited entry.

CHAPTER 39

THE FINISHED PAPER
(MANUSCRIPT PREPARATION)

Your final concern is to produce a paper that is handsome and that meets commonly accepted standards for the format of research papers. In the actual preparation of your manuscript, check the following points:

▣ FORMAT

Paper   Type on plain white 8½ × 11" typing paper. Separate the pages and remove the perforated edges from computer paper.

Typeface   On a computer, use a standard #12 size typeface (not italics, all capitals, or large print).

Page numbers   Number each page after the first. If possible, use a *header* that includes your last name and the page number.

Spacing   Double-space the entire paper, including the Works Cited page and any long quotations that have been set off. You should get approximately twenty-seven lines per page.

Margins   Use margins of 1 to 1½ inches on all four sides. Do not justify (line up) the right margins.

Paragraphing   You have two choices in paragraph indentation, depending on your teacher's preferences: You can indent the first line of each paragraph five spaces. Or you can use block format (no indentation of the first line) and add an extra return between paragraphs. Do not mix these two formats.

Page endings   Be sure that you leave a sufficient bottom margin. Do not end the page with only half a line of type unless you are at the end of a paragraph. Instead, continue to the right margin. It is fine to end the page in midsentence.

Spaces around punctuation   Be sure you have:

- One space after commas, colons, and semicolons. Although it is now correct to have only one space after periods, exclamation points, and question marks, most teachers still prefer two.

- No spaces before any punctuation marks except opening parentheses and quotation marks. Do not begin a line with a period or comma.

Word division   In general, avoid dividing words at the end of a line; if you must divide an unusually long word, divide between syllables (as indicated in a dictionary).

Long quotations   Do not use quotation marks for long quotations (those taking three lines or more). Instead, set them off by indenting every line ten spaces on the left. Don't indent from the right.

Headings   In a short paper, headings may seem disruptive and make the paper choppy. If you decide, for a longer paper, that headings are important, limit yourself to one level of heading, centered or aligned with the left margin and typed in capitals and lowercase. You can make headings stand out by underlining or boldfacing them, or you can use a contrasting typeface.

Illustrations   If you plan to insert graphics or illustrations into the body of your paper, be sure to leave space for them as you type. Ideally, first tape your illustration onto a page and then photocopy that page. You will have a cleaner and perhaps even sharper illustration.

Coversheet or title page   You must include with your paper:

- Your title (centered vertically and horizontally if using a coversheet)

- Your name, the course, the professor's name, and the date (in the bottom right-hand corner of coversheet)

Some teachers like coversheets; others prefer that you put the title and other information on the first page of your manuscript. Follow your teacher's preference.

Submiting electronically   Save your document in RTF (rich text format). Number each paragraph in brackets on the left of the first line, and then skip two spaces. Skip a line between paragraphs. Put an underscore before and after any title that must be underlined. Any necessary punctuation goes after the underscore.

☐ Assembling Your Paper

Once your paper is typed, there is a conventional order for assembling it:

- Coversheet (if required)

- Abstract (if required)—a one-page summary of your thesis and main points

- Outline, including thesis statement (if required)

- The paper (do not repeat the title on page one if you have a coversheet)

- Works Cited page

- Appendix (if you have one)

- Supplementary Bibliography (an optional list of sources you read but did not cite). Use the same format as for the Works Cited page.

Staple your paper once in the upper left-hand corner. Do not put your paper into a binder or folder unless asked to do so. (Many teachers find binders cumbersome.)

☐ Eliminating Keyboarding and Printing Errors

Typographical errors and computer glitches, even though they don't show a lack of knowledge on your part, do show a lack of care. Find them and fix them. To guard against them:

- Make sure all of your deletions got deleted; check adjacent letters and spaces to be sure they did not get messed up in the process.

- Make sure all of your insertions got inserted; again, check adjacent letters and spaces.

- Correct all printer errors. Even though the machine made the mistake, you're responsible for fixing it.

■ FINAL PROOFREADING

No matter how pressed you are, do not submit a final copy that you have not proofread thoroughly. Even at the last minute, make neat corrections with a *black* pen rather than hand in a paper with uncorrected errors.

- First read your entire paper on the screen, page by page, if you typed on a computer. Check tops and bottoms of pages for spacing or omission problems.

- Use the spellcheck one last time to be certain you have not made new errors in insertions.

- After you have printed out your hard copy, proofread for errors the spellcheck won't catch, such as *it's* for *its* and *there* for *their*. Remember, the spellcheck will only catch misspelled words—not words used incorrectly.

- Proofread your hard copy several times, paying special attention to the errors you know you usually make.

- Make any necessary handwritten corrections on your paper as neatly as possible. This is not the stage to add or cross out material, unless absolutely necessary.

CHAPTER 40

IN A CRUNCH 6
(THE ELEVENTH HOUR)

☐ CONCENTRATE FIRST ON LARGE-SCALE REVISION

Make sure that your strongest points stand out:

- What do you most want to show your reader?
- What is the best evidence you have found?

Be certain that these points have prominent positions in your paper and that they are clearly explained.

☐ IF YOUR PAPER IS TOO SHORT

Don't fudge on the word count. You should have approximately 250 words per page, approximately twenty-seven lines per page. Do not insert chunks directly out of your sources to make your paper longer. *Do* add your own comments to quotations and facts you have taken from sources. Remember that most of the paper should be in your own words.

☐ PERK UP YOUR STYLE BY REWRITING YOUR INTRODUCTION AND CONCLUSION

You may have limited revising time at this point. Use whatever time you have to make both your introduction and your conclusion more interesting to read. Your beginning and end can make a big difference in the overall reaction to your paper.

☐ CHECK YOUR DOCUMENTATION DETAILS

Again, this is not a step you can overlook. Take one last look at each of your citations and at each entry on your Works Cited page. Make sure that form, spelling, and punctuation are correct in these two essential areas.

☐ PROOFREAD YOUR FINAL PAPER AND MAKE CORRECTIONS

Even at the last minute, make neat handwritten corrections with a black pen. Use correction fluid if necessary. Indicate deletions by drawing one neat line through the words; indicate insertions by using a carat mark (^) for a few words or an asterisk (*) for longer sentences written elsewhere on the page.

EPILOGUE

GOING FURTHER

Collaborative Research
(*Working with a Team*)

Research Papers about Literature
(*Incorporating Critics' Ideas into Your Own Analysis*)

An Extended Research Project
(*Working Independently*)

EPILOGUE

COLLABORATIVE RESEARCH
(WORKING WITH A TEAM)

At some point during your college education, you may be assigned a group project. And once out in the professional world where much research is conducted by teams, you'll probably find yourself involved in a variety of collaborative projects.

◼ GENERAL PRINCIPLES FOR WORKING IN A GROUP

Let Go of Total Control

- **Be open to the variety of ways different people contribute.** Some people like to take charge and immediately have an idea of what to do. Some are quiet but do excellent work. Some add fun and life to the process. Some care about getting details right. Some are eager to help with the basics—typing, for instance.

- **Negative criticism causes not only bad feelings but poor work.** Avoid being picky; often a problem that bothers you will get solved in the course of discussion. An idea that at first sounds out of line could be important. Stay positive toward each member of the group, give each person time to speak, and the group will work far more creatively, happily, and successfully.

Exercise Patience

- **People work at different rates.** To benefit from the whole group, fast workers shouldn't rush those whose ideas need time.

- **Realize that time "wasted" is not always wasted.** Exchanging news, having coffee, arguing over the same point twice is not really wasting time. Through these processes a group becomes a team and more of the group become involved. To work well in a group, you need to tolerate some degree of chaos.

■ TIPS FOR WORKING IN A GROUP

Here are some practical steps that a group can take from the outset to ensure that the members work together smoothly and effectively:

- **Take advantage of having a group to work with.** Meet regularly and frequently to exchange ideas and to help each other. Take time to build a community spirit. Make sure that everyone is participating.

- **Agree in advance about how the group will handle conflict and disagreements.** At first the whole group is usually excited about the project; then the inevitable disagreements begin to seep in. Plan for clashes ahead of time by agreeing to immediately, openly, and honestly bring the problem before the group. Stay away from gossip and backbiting.

- **Decide on the division of labor.** Will each person be completely in charge of one aspect of the project, or will everyone share responsibility? Talk over how each group member works, and what each likes to do. List all necessary steps, and then let people volunteer for them. Make sure that the group reviews the final list so that everyone feels that the division of work is both fair and practical.

- **Decide how you will handle expenses.** As soon as possible, make a list of expected expenses, and then add a small sum for unexpected ones. All members must agree on the expenses ahead of time and be willing and able to pay their share.

- **Agree on intermediate deadlines.** Decide together when everyone will bring a certain amount of work to discuss. Even when you intend to divide the writing of the final report, seeing each other's work at key points will help you to unify the project and use everyone's ideas.

- **Write separately, in most cases, then come together.** The style is often disastrous when you compose sentences together. Discuss possible revisions until you discover what you all want to say. This process takes time. Then one person should write the new draft.

- **Be flexible.** Be prepared to modify the original plan if it is not working. For example, one member may have been working harder and longer than anyone else with not much to show for it. The whole group might decide that this person needs help or that this part of the project needs to be reconsidered.

RESEARCH PAPERS ABOUT LITERATURE

(INCORPORATING CRITICS' IDEAS INTO YOUR OWN ANALYSIS)

One of the major differences between a literary research paper and a traditional documented paper is that, in a literary paper, your main focus is on the text—or work of art—itself. The research takes second place to your own close reading or observation of the piece you are writing about.

You can adapt the methods described here for writing about other arts such as film, music, painting, dance, and architecture.

■ PLANNING YOUR PROJECT

Your First Step Always Is to Read the Literature Itself

First, carefully read the primary text—the work of literature you are studying. Your first reading should be a time to enjoy the text, to respond without the pressure to come up with answers or ideas.

A good idea is to keep a *reading journal*. Whenever your reading leads you into a line of thought, note the number of the page you are on and take a few minutes to write down your thoughts. Later you can search through your journal for your best ideas.

Be Clear About the Assignment

Make sure you understand what you are being asked to do: Are you being asked to compare your ideas to those of critics? Are you being asked to find out about the historical context surrounding a piece of work? The specific assignment will dictate the kind of sources you should choose.

Freewrite before Doing Research

Before reading any critics, freewrite about the topic, if your teacher has given you one; otherwise write about your thoughts and feelings in response to the reading. Write out several ideas about the assignment that you might emphasize in an essay.

◻ CONDUCTING THE RESEARCH

Choose Several Critics to Read

Not all critical studies are equal. To find the best critics to read, a good place to start is with the introduction and any list of recommended readings in the edition of the work you are studying. You can also look at recommended sources in anthologies (such as *The Norton Anthology of English Literature*). The most complete listings of books and articles about literature are in the *MLA* (Modern Language Association) *Bibliography*. Also your professor may guide you to the best critical studies.

Read the Critics Carefully and Critically

Take notes on their main ideas. If you are reading just one chapter of a book, take time to read the preface and introduction so you will understand the critic's approach.

Look for ideas that correspond to your own experience of the work. Be open to reconsidering and refining your first impressions as you do your research, even changing them completely at times. But remember that your experience as a reader has value and must be the heart of your essay.

◻ PLANNING AND WRITING YOUR ESSAY

When you've finished your research, your next step is to formulate the main ideas your paper will emphasize. Decide which ideas you feel most committed to and are most able to back up with evidence from the text and from your research. You will need to patiently reread the literature itself, searching for evidence that supports or changes your ideas.

Avoid Plot Summary

Organize your essay around *your* ideas, not by following the plot or chronology of the piece you are writing about. Your goal is to show how your ideas are supported by the text and by your research.

Use Evidence to Support Your Assertions

Make a list of the main points you would like to establish. Under each point, list the evidence or examples that will best demonstrate it. In literary essays, *evidence* means:

- Specific quotations and details from the *primary* source, the literature itself; anything that another person could observe readily when you point it out.

- Facts and ideas you have gathered from *secondary* sources, critics and historians.

The majority of your evidence should come from your primary source, which you can then support with information from your secondary sources.

Incorporate Evidence Gracefully

Do not ever organize your paper by summarizing one secondary source at a time. Nor should you use too many *direct quotations* from either primary or secondary sources. Instead, use *paraphrase* and *summary*.

- Never put in a quotation or fact that is not helping to clarify the point of the paragraph you are writing.

- Avoid using very long quotations; use a number of brief ones instead.

- Make clear why you have used a particular quotation.

- Clarify abstract ideas and literary terms with concrete examples and quotations.

For general advice about incorporating evidence, see Chapter 24; for specific skills of quotation, paraphrase, and summary, see Chapters 25–27.

▪ Conventions of Literary Essays

Your Title

You must make up your own title, not merely use the title of the work. You can incorporate the work's title into your own.

> The Vision of Hope in Langston Hughes's "Mother to Son"
>
> The Use of Color in Stephen Crane's
> <u>The Red Badge of Courage</u>

Identifying Author and Title

You should use the author's full name the first time you refer to him or her; after that, use only the last name without Ms. or Mr.

Underline or italicize titles of books, plays, films, periodicals, and other long works. Place quotation marks around titles of poems, stories, essays, and other short works.

Early in your essay, identify the author and title of the work you are analyzing.

> "Mother to Son," by Langston Hughes, portrays a strong woman whose many hardships have never caused her to give up on life.
>
> In <u>The Red Badge of Courage</u>, Stephen Crane uses shades and hues of color as if he were an artist painting a canvas.

Note: A comma or a period, if needed following a title, goes *inside* quotation marks.

Use Present Tense

In writing your paper, use the present tense, the most graceful tense for referring to a poem or story. Even if the author uses past tense in discussing the story—"So that is marriage, Lily thought, a man and a woman looking at a girl throwing a ball"—you should use present tense in discussing it:

> When she turns and sees the Ramseys, Lily Briscoe thinks, "So that is marriage [. . .] a man and a woman looking at a girl throwing a ball."

Note that the original verb, *thought* becomes *thinks* as you write in present tense when describing the story. Also notice the ellipsis that indicates you have left out "Lily thought."

Quoting Poetry

When you quote more than one line of poetry, indent the whole quotation ten spaces from the left margin. The point is to reproduce the same line endings that the poet used:

> Well, son, I'll tell you,
> Life for me ain't been no crystal stair.

When a line of poetry is too long to fit on a line of your paper, indent the turnover line an additional three spaces.

When quoting a few words of poetry that include a line break, use a slash mark to show where the poet's line ends:

> Emily Dickinson describes the coldness of death creeping "like frost upon a glass,/till all the scene be gone."

Page References

In your paper, indicate the location of each quotation from your primary source by putting the page number in parentheses following the quotation (see Chapter 31, "Parenthetical Citation"). For a poem, give the line number; for the Bible, give chapter and verse; for a play, give act and scene (and line number, if listed).

> The first chapter of Hawthorne's The Scarlet Letter puns on the mix of church and state in the "steeple-crowned hats" of the Puritans (35).

> In "Mother to Son," by Langston Hughes, the speaker claims that "Life for me ain't been no crystal stair" (2).

> "There shall be weeping and gnashing of teeth" (Luke 14:28).

> In The Winter's Tale, Shakespeare includes a beautiful catalog of the "flow'rs o' th' spring" (4.4.113).

When quoting from or referring to an idea from a critic, always mention the critic's name, and give the source when appropriate:

> Eudora Welty, in the foreword of To the Lighthouse, says that, in this novel, Virginia Woolf "has shown us the shape of the human spirit" (xii).

Bibliographical Information

You will need a Works Cited page following the format in Chapters 34 and 35. Include an entry for every source you cited within the paper, including the edition of the literary text that you have used.

> Hughes, Langston. "Mother to Son." Selected Poems of Langston Hughes. New York: Knopf, 1970. 187.

If the book was originally published in an edition different from yours, put the original date of publication after the title:

> Woolf, Virginia. To the Lighthouse. 1927. San Diego: Harcourt, 1981.

If you used a poem or short story in an anthology or an introduction or a preface from a book, you need to include a citation for the author and specific short work you referred to, as well as all the information for the book, including the pages covered (see page 142).

> Meltzer, Richard. "The Aesthetics of Rock." Penguin Book of Rock & Roll Writing. Ed. Clinton Heylin. New York: Viking, 1992. 81–87.

> Welty, Eudora. Foreword. To the Lighthouse. By Virginia Woolf. San Diego: Harcourt, 1981. vii–xii.

An Extended Research Project
(Working Independently)

At some point in college, you may undertake a long-term research project—perhaps as a thesis in your major, as an independent study program, or as an option in a course.

Doing an extended research project will take you progressively deeper into your subject and make you an expert in it. Choose a subject that you feel wholeheartedly committed to and something you can live with for an interval of time.

■ Planning Your Project

It's possible to survive a month-long project on a topic you dislike, but a long-term project requires motivation, best found in selecting a topic you care about.

- Brainstorm and freewrite to find a topic that you really want to study.

- Develop a long-term plan for your project.

- Consult with your instructor early and regularly.

Previewing Your Research

Once you've settled on a topic you feel really energetic about, the next step is to do several hours of general reading to gain an overview of the literature available in the field. Consult a recent encyclopedia for a comprehensive summary, and then browse through a few up-to-date books or articles. Look for bibliographies and recommended reading.

Start to compile a *working bibliography*, a list of books and articles on your subject. The purpose of the working bibliography is to be certain that sufficient reference materials are available for your subject. Gather a variety of materials—popular as well as scholarly articles and books, videos, government documents, and so forth. Be certain your sources are not obsolete. Write down all bibliographical information for each source and a brief summary of it. These personal summaries will come in handy when you go further into your research.

Writing a Research Proposal

You may be asked to submit a research proposal. In writing one, you will discover whether you are committed to your field of research. Writing it will also help you focus on the goals that you hope to meet in conducting your research.

Introduction   To begin the proposal, give a general introduction to your topic. Write several paragraphs, targeting the material to your reader's level of expertise. The introduction can also include why you have an interest in this subject.

The heart of the proposal   State specifically what you hope to accomplish in your research. Clearly state each of your research goals (there should be several) and briefly explain what steps you plan to take in accomplishing each of them.

Include a working bibliography   Attach to the end of your proposal a list of sources which you plan to use; this will give your adviser an overview of the literature available on the subject. But be selective; include only those sources you have found most helpful and expect to use in your research. Use the same format for a working bibliography as you do for a Works Cited page.

■ During the Project

Begin writing as soon as you begin reading.   You should not wait to finish your research before you write the paper. Instead, write parts of the paper as you read, even though you do not know the shape of your final essay and may not use much of what you first write. It's also a good idea to keep a section of your notebook just for notes to yourself about your sense of the project and where it is leading.

Schedule frequent meetings with your adviser.   Stay in close touch with your adviser to be certain you are on the right track. Ask your adviser to comment on different parts of your paper as you draft them.

Read a few sources on a contrasting but related topic.   For example, look for an article on renovation of the New York subway system in the 1980s to give a fresh perspective on your study of their design in the 1890s. Or balance your study of AIDS with an article on another fatal epidemic, such as the swine flu or polio. Even if you can't use this new information, reading a different approach will broaden your perspective.

Talk about your project with others.   One problem with long-term projects is that they can be isolating. Discuss your findings with friends, not so much to get their ideas as to articulate your own.

Expect to revise a number of times.   Put your work into a computer early in the process and store it in short documents rather than one long one. Long papers in particular go through more drafts than you might expect. Revision will entail not only touch-ups but complete changes of emphasis. Allow more time proportionately for revising a long project than you usually do for the revision process.

◼ AFTER THE PROJECT

Now that you have some expertise in your field, share what you've learned with others through writing and speaking. You can:

- Write a letter to the editor of your local newspaper.
- Offer to give an informal talk at your library.
- Share your findings with a discussion group on the Internet.
- Write an article and send it out for publication.
- Apply for a job or an internship in the field you've studied.

If you have completed an extended research project, you have learned what it means to know a subject well enough to speak and write about it with authority. The skills you have developed can be used to conduct research on any subject, at any time, in any situation for the rest of your life.

APPENDIX

Two Sample Student Papers:

- *Student Paper Using MLA Style*
- *Student Paper Using APA Style*

A List of Important Sources

TWO SAMPLE STUDENT PAPERS

The following sample research papers were written by first-semester composition students at Nassau Community College. We have made necessary changes only in format and documentation but have left other elements of the papers (logic, organization, style, and use of evidence) as written.

STUDENT PAPER USING MLA STYLE

Dirty Times

Jenifer Franceschi-Wood
English 102 FA
Dr. J. R. Silverman
20 Apr. 1998

Franceshi-Wood

The American people have an obsession with
personal cleanliness; that is why the market
for soaps, shampoos, and deodorants is such a
good one. No matter what the marketing strategy,
such products will always sell. It is not a   5
coincidence that to be clean and well deodorized
has become especially desirable since the
invention of television. Surely, the last forty
or fifty years have been particularly well
deodorized because television tells us that   10
being clean and smelling good is desirable.

However, long before television and the
mass media, we were a rather dirty bunch of
human beings. Today, we take for granted a
simple shower or bath with soap and fresh   15
clean water, but in the past keeping clean
was not quite so simple. In fact, a clean
and deodorized America would be shocked at
how seldom our recent ancestors bathed. After
all, people didn't always have deodorant   20
and soap, so sometimes plain water had to
suffice (plain water that was not clean in
and of itself, to say the least). How did
they do it? How did they keep clean in medieval
times and in the Victorian Age? They didn't do   25
it very well, and there is an enormous difference
between the personal habits of the rich and
the poor back in those times.

Franchesi-Wood 2

Medieval England was a dangerous place to
live. Frances and Joseph Gies explain that often   30
the plague was rampant and the person who was
lucky enough to live past childhood usually did
not live past the age of forty-five (121).
Medieval peasants rarely if ever bathed, and one
can only wonder if the spread of the plague and   35
other diseases could have been curbed with the use
of a little personal hygiene. Gathering the water
was a great deal of work, so unless it was
specified for cooking, it was not seen as worth
the effort. Gies and Gies tell how a family of   40
five would take their baths about once a month and
usually use the same bath water in succession. A
barrel with the top removed served as a bathing
vessel (93). On a particularly dirty day, say, if
a peasant was covered in mud from working in the   45
fields, he or she might wash with some plain water
to get rid of the grime (Buehr 134). Farm animals
moved freely in and out of the hovels and slept a
matter of a few feet away from the occupants of
the home (Howarth 12). When tidying up the house   50
it was normal to sweep up animal dung along with
the rest of the dirt on the floor (Gies and Gies
92-93). In towns, some people bathed in public
bath houses called "stews." Stews were well known
for having open nudity between the sexes, and   55
loose women could frequently be found there
(Buehr 134). No wonder there was so much death
from disease.

Franchesi-Wood 3

The rich lived slightly differently in
medieval times. Some of the rich saw baths as   60
having medicinal qualities. King John washed
in "sweet green herbs" with "five or six sponges
to sit upon" and rinsed with rosewater
(Hassall 210). A contemporary record of these
procedures explains that first one would "boil   65
leaves and herbs" and then

> Throw them hot into a vessel and put
> your lord over it and let him endure
> it for a while . . . whatever disease,
> grievance or pain ye be vexed with,   70
> this medicine will surely make you
> whole. . . . (qtd. in Hassall 211)

Apparently the rich had the luxury of
using baths as a cure for ills while the poor
used them sparingly. Still, rich and poor of   75
medieval times were both afflicted with insects
and vermin. It was a rare person who wasn't
tormented by lice and fleas (Collis 10). One
can only wonder if this was because of the
lack of real soap rather than herbs & leaves.   80
Charles Panati reports that soap dates back
to the Phoenicians in 600 BC, but soap production
"virtually came to a halt" in the Middle Ages
when the Christian Church forbade "exposing
the flesh, even to bathe" (218).   85

I'm not sure what happened to "cleanliness is next to godliness," but even before the Church made modesty more important than getting rid of dirt, it was clear that the English society didn't care much for sanitation. The Romans had introduced the concepts of sewage disposal and providing a clean water supply for drinking and bathing to England in 43 AD, but Quennell and Quennell write that "Incredible as it may sound, no real advance was made for 1400 years; from the early fifth century until the beginning of the nineteenth century people were not concerned with Public Health" (88).

Things did not get much better—at least for the poor—in Victorian England. Many people think that the Victorians were prudish about their bodies and therefore would not allow themselves to go unwashed. This is only partially true. In Victorian England the well-to-do were the ones who kept stately homes and wore fine clothes. The wealthy had frequent baths and washed daily with water and soap (Childers 406). A basin was kept in the bedroom and every morning it was filled with fresh water to wash with. When the regular bath was taken, a high-backed tub called a "hip bath" was placed on the bedroom floor over some towels to catch any water that splashed out. The servants carried fresh hot water up in metal cans. The whole process was laborious, but the

Victorians enjoyed it a great deal. At this   115
point there were bathrooms, but most wealthy
Victorians preferred to bathe in their rooms.
The thought of sharing bathing facilities with
other family members was repugnant to them
(Quennell and Quennell 71).   120

    The poor were not so lucky in Victorian
England. Since the poorer class accounted for
the masses in Victorian England, a great many
people lived in filth and muck. According to
E. Royston Pike, it was normal for two or three   125
families to live in one room (at a lodging house)
and to urinate and defecate in a pail in the
center of the room. Beds were always filthy
and full of worms and insects; people were
plagued by lice and fleas (Pike 298-99). The   130
rooms in the lodging houses were usually
unventilated and waterless. In 1849, medical
reports explained how leaking pipes released
contaminated water into the London reservoir;
thus a whole neighborhood could be contaminated   135
by water containing raw sewage (qtd. in
Pike 306). The 1850 *London News* reported
"routine city flooding when the Thames
'backed up'" (qtd. in Gayman). Sometimes
water lines would run through cemeteries and   140
pick up decomposing animal matter (Pike 281).
When the people did bathe, either the water was
black with dirt and sewage or dripped sparingly

from a pipe that a whole village waited in line
to use (Pike 79). Ironically, the lodging houses   145
would not admit people unless they had cleaned
their feet (Pike 298).

It is entirely possible that the obsession
with cleanliness that we know today stems from
the modern knowledge that filth breeds disease.   150
However, I think that this knowledge has evolved
into neuroticism. It is not enough to be thin and
beautiful or rich and handsome. One must be fresh
and clean too. That brings to mind a commercial
for a deodorant that I saw just recently. A young   155
woman ruminates on how gross it is when she gets
really close and a guy smells bad. I think this
is why the producers of that deodorant make so
much money; they shame us into buying their
product. The poet Galway Kinnell calls   160
advertisers "anti-prostitutes" because they
"loathe human flesh for money" (43).

Still, when I walk into a store or a
classroom and my nose is invaded by the stench of
someone's body odor, I cannot help but wonder if   165
he or she has seen that commercial or passed by
the deodorant aisle of the supermarket lately. It
occurs to me that television has gotten me too.
Perhaps if I were back in Victorian or medieval
times, I wouldn't care so much about that   170
person's body odor; but then again, neither
of us would have much choice.

Works Cited

Buehr, Walter. When Towns Had Walls: Life in a
    Medieval English Town. New York: Crowell, 1970.

Childers, Joseph W. "Observation and Representation:
    Mr. Chadwick Writes the Poor." Victorian
    Studies 37 (1994) 405-31.

Collis, Louise. Memoirs of a Medieval Woman: The Life
    and Times of Margery Kempe. New York: Perennial,
    1983.

Gayman, Mary. "The Badd Olde Days." Cleaner. n.d. Cole
    Pub. [Three Lakes, WI]. 25 Oct. 1997 <http://klingon.
    util.utexas.edu/londonsewers/londontext3.html>.

Gies, Frances, and Joseph Gies. Life in a Medieval
    Village. New York: Harper, 1990.

Hassall, W. O. Medieval England as Viewed by
    Contemporaries. New York: Harper, 1967.

Howarth, Sarah. Medieval Places. Brookfield,
    CT: Millbrook, 1992.

Kinnell, Galway. "The Dead Shall Be Raised
    Incorrectible." Book of Nightmares. Boston:
    Houghton, 1971. 39-43.

Panati, Charles. Extraordinary Origins of Everyday
    Things. New York: Harper, 1987.

Pike, E. Royston. Golden Times: Human Documents of
    the Victorian Age. New York: Praeger, 1967.

Quennell, Marjorie, and C. H. B. Quennell. A History
    of Everyday Things in England: The Rise of
    Industrialism. London: B. T. Batsford, 1933.

STUDENT PAPER USING APA STYLE

Sleeping Pills: Help or Hindrance?

Steven Pangiotidis
English 101 HD/
Sociology 201 HA
Professor Ferris
Term Report
11/23/97

Pangiotidis

Abstract: Sleeping pills are harmful drugs that are often taken for sleep deprivation. They have become a real epidemic, and the statistics to prove it are amazing. Overprescribing is the main cause of the problem. Doctors are prescribing   5
unneeded medications, but that's not the only reason for the crisis. Many people with sleep disorders are abusing these drugs and can't overcome their addictions. They take the drugs because they feel a psychological need as well   10
as to sleep better. But the effects of sleeping pills are very harmful. They reduce the activity of the brain and nervous system, and can cause both mental and physical addiction. An overdose can cause coma or death. Besides being ineffective   15
in curing the sleep disorder, they can often make the problem worse. Until doctors stop overprescribing and many of the products are taken off the store shelves, the epidemic will continue. In the future, if we can get all our   20
facts straight on sleeping pills, we can turn the epidemic around.

Pangiotidis

Thesis: Sleeping pills—widely overprescribed—are not the answer to sleep deprivation because they do little to help the situation, and their side effects, which include addiction, can be very harmful.

Topic Outline

   I. Introduction

      A. Choice of many

      B. Definition

  II. Long-term sleeping pill epidemic

      A. Government statistics

      B. Overprescribing

      C. General Problems

 III. Discussion of Problem

      A. Addiction

      B. Other Dangers

      C. Ineffectiveness

  IV. Solutions

      A. Stopping overprescribing

      B. Taking products off supermarket shelves

      C. Finding the cause of sleeplessness

      D. Eliminating the abuse

         1. Overcoming addiction

         2. Poem about need for sleeping pills

   V. Conclusion

      A. Publishing facts

      B. Turnaround of epidemic

Pangiotidis

Sleeplessness is not a new disease, but it
does seem to be a growing epidemic these days.
People who suffer from sleep deprivation try many
different options to go to sleep. Some exercise,
others eat, and some even count sheep. Those who   5
can afford it, go to a sleep laboratory for a
proper diagnosis. However, many take the low
road and swallow sleeping pills.

Sleeping pills are drugs used to calm people
down or make them sleep. All sleep aids   10
"specifically depress brain activity . . . and
make people drowsy" (Zimmerman, 1993, pp. 871-72).
However, sleeping pills—widely overprescribed—are
not the answer to sleep deprivation because they
do little to help the situation, and their side   15
effects, which include addiction, can be very
harmful. An overdose can cause coma—or even death.

The sleeping pill epidemic has existed for
some time now, but only recently have we finally
begun to realize it. In the United States alone,   20
as early as 1964 (the first year such data was
collected), "over 32 million prescriptions for
sleeping pills were written" (Trubo, p. 74). By
now, the numbers must be staggering. Dr. Samuel
Dunkell (1994), Director of the Insomnia Medical   25
Services in New York City, estimated that about
one-third of our entire population experiences
sleep difficulties. A large number of these people
receive prescriptions for sleeping pills and

masses of others turn to "over-the-counter   30
preparations, street and recreational drugs,
and alcoholic nightcaps . . . for sleep" (p. 94).
According to government statistics about
30 percent of sleeping pill prescriptions are
given to people whose problem is "primarily   35
psychological in origin"; another 25 percent
go to those with medical conditions that won't
respond to sleeping pills, while still another
18 percent go to patients "with ill defined
or vague symptoms that usually don't require   40
drug treatment" (Hales, 1981, pp. 281–82). As
long ago as 1973, Dr. Ernest L. Hartmann
found that "As many as four out of five
sleep pill prescriptions are inappropriate
or ineffective" (p. 41).   45

A few of the mind-boggling statistics
concerning sleeping pills have been compiled
by Donald R. Sweeney (1989). He said that
sleeping medications are "the most widely used
class of drugs" in this country and that in   50
the U.S. alone, we consume "approximately
600 tons of sleep medications" (p. 232).

Here's the kicker: In many cases these pills
don't work, make the problem worse, or result
in serious side effects. Even if these drugs do   55
help you sleep, it isn't a " 'good' sleep"
because these medications "distort the normal sleep
patterns . . . and give you a 'hangover' feeling
the next morning" (DiGeronimo, 1997, pp. 84–86).   60

Some people take large amounts of sleeping pills to escape tension, as well as to sleep better, which has a lot to do with the alarming statistics. Such doses produce intoxication similar to that caused by alcohol. Users' speech   65 becomes slurred, and their coordination and judgment become poor. People who regularly take large doses of sleeping pills develop an addiction. "When addicted people try to stop using the pills," says Hartmann (1973), "they   70 suffer convulsions, body twitchings, and severe nervousness" (p. 43). Even worse, Hartmann pointed out that sudden withdrawal from the drugs can cause death. Addicts can end their dependence on sleeping pills only by gradually   75 reducing the amount they take.

Although sleeping pills have become safer in recent years since most barbiturates have been replaced with benzodiazepines (Graber, 1995, p. 106), the dangers and discomforts of sleeping   80 pills are still very real. Zimmerman (1993) pointed out these risks:

- Fatal overdoses, particularly if combined with alcohol or any medications affecting the nervous system   85
- Dizziness and blurred or double vision
- Loss of appetite; nausea and vomiting
- Fatigue; mood changes, such as anxiety and even delirium (p. 873).

    The irony is that with all these risks,   90
sleeping pills don't work all that well. Treating
a sleep disorder with these drugs may produce
sleep for a few days, or even a few weeks, but in
the long run they are just making the problem
worse. When I interviewed Dr. Michael J. Thorpy   95
(September 27, 1997), he said, "As a lasting
solution to a sleep problem, sleeping pills
do little, if any, good. And they can do
considerable harm." Dr. Nathaniel Kleitman (1990),
a sleep therapist, put it best when he said   100
that "in a sense sleeping pills are like throat
lozenges, which soothe the irritation but do not
cure the cough" (qtd. in Toufexis p. 79).

    What are the solutions to this epidemic?
One way to avoid the dangers of sleeping pills   105
is to end the senseless prescribing. Doctors
should stop misusing their authority, and
when a patient asks for medication, they
shouldn't be so quick to pick up their pens.
First they should examine the patient and   110
see if he or she really needs the drugs.
Then, and only then, should they even consider
writing out the slip. Klinkenborg (1997) reported
in the <u>New York Times</u> that, in the United States,
these powerful drugs can be obtained only   115
with a prescription. I disagree because I
think that many of these drugs are still
out there in the supermarket aisles where

depressed teenagers, or anyone for that matter,
can have easy access to them. I also think that   120
many of these dangerous drugs are still sitting
out on store shelves disguised as cold remedies
and other medications—for example, NyQuil, "the
nighttime sniffling, sneezing, coughing,
aching, stuffy head, fever [so you can go into   125
a coma] medicine." Once, for a cold, I took
some NyQuil, which contains an antihistamine,
and it put me into such a deep, long sleep, that
when I woke up (which seemed like weeks later),
I didn't remember anything.   130

      In a recent discussion group (September 12,
1997), Sarah Gale reported that she "went from
herbal remedies to NyQuil, sommenex [sic] and
finally double doses of sleeping pills" without
success, until she finally cured her anxiety   135
about sleep through hypnosis. She recommended that
people find out <u>why</u> they can't sleep. Her experience
is a perfect example of what is wrong with
searching for the perfect medication. People
can be helped to get a good night's rest if   140
the reason for their sleeplessness is treated.

      One thing I can do, as well as other
people with sleep problems, is to stay away from
sleeping pills. In my interview with Dr. Thorpy
(September 27, 1997), he said that "the only   145
people who can change this problem are the ones
who are having trouble sleeping." There should
be more doctors like Dr. Thorpy, who always

discourages his patients from taking any

sleeping pills.   150

   But many people just can't overcome their

addiction to these pills, even when they know

perfectly well that they really don't work in the

long run. The following poem, written by Ryah

Goodman (1981), reveals the deep psychological   155

needs that make a person turn to sleeping pills:

>   The light within me clicks,
>
>   Who put out the light?
>
>   It is dark.
>
>   I am alone, afraid.   160
>
>   Mother, Mother,
>
>   I can't sleep.
>
>   My mother does not come.
>
>   My mother is dead.
>
>   One pill,   165
>
>   Two pills,
>
>   Three pills,
>
>   Mother me, pills. (qtd. in Hales, p. 130)

   In conclusion, I don't think that sleeping

pills are the answer to our sleep problems. They   170

rarely help; in fact, they usually make the matter

worse. Dr. Thorpy (personal communication,

September 27, 1997) said,

>   As a rule, I am not enthusiastic about
>
>   the use of these products in sleep   175
>
>   deprivation. Besides being ineffective,
>
>   especially

in long-term use, they can cause nausea,
vomiting, and other side effects and they
usually do not treat the basic psychological
problem.   180
    I can only hope that I'm not the only one to
learn these facts and have a better perspective
on this topic. Perhaps in the future we can learn
to make the right decisions when coming across
sleeping pills. We all have to get the necessary   185
facts in order to do our part in turning this
crisis around and stopping the senseless abuse
of these very dangerous drugs.

References

DiGeronimo, T. F. (1997). Insomnia: 50 essential things to do. New York: Penguin.

Dunkell, S. (1994). Goodbye insomnia, hello sleep. Birch Lane.

Gale, S. F. (1997, September 12). I solved my sleep disorder! Posting to alt.support.sleep-disorder. Retrieved October 13, 1997 from the World Wide Web: http://xp10dejanews.com/getdoc.xp

Graber, R. (1995). How to get a good night's sleep. Minneapolis: Chronimed.

Hales, D. (1981). The complete book of sleep. Boston: Addison-Wesley.

Hartmann, E. L. (1973). The function of sleep. New Haven: Yale U P.

Klinkenborg, V. (1997, 5 January). Awakening to sleep. New York Times sec. 7: pp. 26+.

Sweeney, D. R. (1989). Overcoming insomnia. New York: Putnam.

Toufexis, A. (1990, December 17). Drowsy America. Time, pp. 78-81.

Trubo, R. (1978). How to get a good night's sleep. Boston: Little, Brown.

Zimmerman, D. R. (1993). Zimmerman's complete guide to nonprescription drugs. Detroit: Gale Research.

A List of Important Sources

Electronic sources listed here are regularly updated on McGraw-Hill's Web site: http://www.mhhe.com/writers

The following lists include the most basic resources. You'll find these reference materials in one or more of the following formats: *print, microfilm,* or *electronic.* Whenever possible, begin your search with the computer because it is comprehensive and takes less time to use. Look for these in your library. They may be listed in a menu of choices on your library's home page, or they may be installed in designated computers. If you do not find the electronic version, use the library catalog to find the print or film version.

Your librarian or teacher may suggest more specific references.

I. GENERAL INDEXES AND OTHER LISTINGS OF BOOKS AND ARTICLES

Bibliographic Index: A Cumulative Bibliography of Bibliographies Lists, by subject, bibliographies published both separately and in books and periodicals.

Books in Print Use this guide to locate books in print by title, author, or subject. See also *Paperback Books in Print.* Also consult the commercial booksellers on the World Wide Web, such as amazon.com, barnesandnoble.com, and bookwire.com.

CARL (Colorado Alliance of Research Libraries at http://uncweb. carl.org) Use their index to find scholarly articles which you can then get at your college library. You don't have to register; the search is free, with copies of articles available for a fee.

Citation indexes (on CD-ROM): *Arts and Humanities Citation Index, Science Citation Index, Social Sciences Citation Index* Each volume has four parts: (1) Permuterm Index—lists specific authors covered; (2) Citation Index— lists where a particular author was cited by other authors that year; (3) Source Index—lists what articles an author published that year; (4) Corporate Index—lists articles published in specific geographical regions.

Cumulative Book Index International bibliography of books published in English worldwide.

ERIC Educational resources (on CD-ROM or at http://ericir.syr.edu) Indexes articles in academic journals regarding teaching methods, curriculum, learning styles, and so forth.

Essay and General Literature Index A guide to individual essays or chapters in books on topics not normally listed in standard indexes or library catalogs.

FirstSearch Includes many of the databases listed here. You can access their Web site at http://gilligan.prod.olc.org if your library subscribes; ask for the authorization numbers and password to use.

Humanities Index (on CD-ROM) Indexes articles from nearly 300 periodicals in the arts, classics, languages, literature, philosophy, and religion.

Infoline (on CD-ROM) Indexes scholarly journals; includes full text.

InfoTrak (on CD-ROM) Includes several indexes listed here.

Magazine Index Plus (on CD-ROM) Indexes over 400 popular and general-interest periodicals.

Medline (on CD-ROM or at http://www.ncbi.nlm.nih.gov/Pub/Med/) Use for topics related to health and medicine.

MLA (Modern Language Association) *International Bibliography* (on CD-ROM) Indexes scholarly articles about language and literature.

National Newspaper Index (on CD-ROM) Indexes articles from five major newspapers: *Christian Science Monitor, Los Angeles Times, New York Times, The Wall Street Journal,* and *Washington Post. Newspapers Online* at http://www.uncq.edu/lib/news provides links to these and many other newspapers all over the world.

New York Times Index: A Book of Record Indexes topics covered by the *New York Times,* annually since 1851. Articles since 1972 are included in the *National Newspaper Index.* For reviews of books, films, or plays, go to the specialized indexes: *New York Times Film Review Index* and so forth.

Periodicals Abstracts (on CD-ROM) Includes summaries of articles.

Readers' Guide to Periodical Literature Indexes articles, by author and subject, from 200 general magazines. Most of the articles since 1972 that are indexed here are in *Magazine Index Plus.*

Sheehy, Eugene P. *Guide to Reference Books* Lists all reference books published in the United States.

Vertical File Index New York: Wilson, 1935–. Indexes, by title and subject, pamphlets on all subjects.

II. GENERAL REFERENCES

Biographies

Biography Index: A Cumulative Index to Biographical Material in Books and Magazines A comprehensive, international listing of biographical information, including major historical figures. Indexed by name and by profession.

Current Biography Gives biographical data about people currently making the news. 1940–.

McGraw-Hill Encyclopedia of World Biography Illustrated, with short biographies of world figures.

New York Times Obituary Index Covers national and international figures; indexed by the year of death.

Who's Who in America. Chicago: Marquis, 1899–present Provides current information about prominent people who are still living. (See also other *Who's Who* and *Who Was Who* guides.)

Directories

BigBook A yellow pages of the Internet   http://www.bigbook.com

Dun's Business Locator (on CD-ROM)

Encyclopedia of Associations Lists, with addresses, professional associations.

Foundation Directory Lists, with addresses, philanthropic foundations and foundations for specialized studies.

Yahoo People Search   http://www.yahoo.com/search/people

Yellowweb   http://www.yellowwwebpages.com/

Encyclopedias

In addition to these general references, look for encyclopedias devoted to your subject—for example, there is a *Baseball Encyclopedia*. New York: Macmillan, 1996.

Collier's Encyclopedia. Good general information source for contemporary subjects.

Encyclopedia Americana Good for scientific and technical topics.

Encyclopedia Britannica (in print, on CD-ROM, or online for a fee) The most definitive, comprehensive encyclopedia. Annual supplement, *Britannica Book of the Year*.

Free Internet Encyclopedia   http://clever.net/cam/encyclopedia.html

Statistical Sources

American Statistical Index (in print and on CD-ROM) A monthly index of all U.S. government statistical publications. Also available at http://www.fedstats.gov or see individual agencies' Web sites.

Bureau of Census Reports Based on census data collected every ten years, reports filled with all sorts of facts about American life are available in print. Selected reports are at http://www.census.gov and on CD-ROM.

County and City Databook (in print and on CD-ROM)

USA Counties (in print and on CD-ROM)

Yearbooks and Almanacs

Facts on File Weekly summaries of U.S. and world news.

Information, Please! Almanac: The New Universe of Information. New York: Houghton. Published annually. Also look for their special almanacs on entertainment, sports, and women.

Famighetti, Robert, ed. *World Almanac and Book of Facts.* Boston: St. Martin's, 1997. An excellent source for statistics in many fields, published annually.

III. SPECIALIZED REFERENCES

Every discipline has specialized references, usually titled with the discipline name plus a word such as *Abstracts, Bibliography, Dictionary, Encyclopedia,* or *Index.* You should use these for some of your early searches. The majority of specialized references are still available only in print, but some—such as *Psychological Abstracts*—will be on CD-ROM installed on computers in the library reference room or available online to library subscribers.

IV. SEARCH TOOLS FOR THE INTERNET

Note: These addresses are regularly updated at
http://www.mhhe.com/writers (McGraw-Hill's Writers' Resource page).

Meta-searchers simultaneously check for your terms among several search
engines. If you have developed a good list of search terms, the most
effective way to begin is with one of these metasearchers.

Dogpile   http://www.dogpile.com
(fun to use, it simultaneously searches through 25 search engines)

Highway 61   http://www.highway61.com
(very fast, it searches the six most popular search engines and arranges the
results by relevance)

Inference Find   http://www.inference.com/infind/
(also very fast and concept oriented, it searches the six top search engines
and organizes the results)

SavvySearch   http://guaraldi.cs.colostate.edu:2000/
(fast and thorough)

USE IT!   http://www.he.net/~kamus/useen.htm
(Unified Search Engine for InTernet—in Italy—includes international sites)

Other Powerful Search Engines

Alta Vista   http://altavista.digital.com
(one of the most comprehensive)

Excite   http://www.excite.com
(includes summaries, sorted by relevance to the topic—offering "more like
this")

Hotbot   http://www.hotbot.com
(fastest and most comprehensive; best for complicated searches and
multimedia topics)

InfoSeek   http://www.infoseek.com
(best for simple searches; also good for refining searches)

Lycos   http://www.lycos.com
(oldest and still one of the best although it doesn't allow searches for
phrases)

NorthernLight   http://www.northernlight.com
(provides folders for organizing your search; also identifies the date of
original posting—often not given on the Web site—and whether a site is a
personal page, commercial, or non-profit; retrieves documents for a fee)

WebCrawler   http://www.webcrawler.com
(one of the fastest)

Subject Lists and Other Important Search Tools

Many of these can be your fastest route to solid information.

The December List   http://www.december.com/cmc/info
(a very important resource with links to information all over the Internet)

Internet Resources MetaIndex
        http://www.ncsa.uiuc.edu/SDG/Software/Mosaic/MetaIndcx.html

Internet Sleuth   http://www.isleuth.com
(includes direct links to some databases not on the Web)

Librarian's Guide to Best Information on the Web
        http://www.sau.edu/CWIS/Internet/Wild/index.htm

Magellan   http://mckinley.com
(good subject search)

The Mother of all Gophers   gopher://gopher.tc.umn.edu
(good for checking for libraries)

Virtual Library
    http://www.w3.org/hypertext/DataSources/bySubject/Overview.html

Yahoo   http://www.yahoo.com
(very fast subject search)

Search Tools for Discussion Groups and Newsgroups

To retrieve threads of conversation from previous discussions
(recommended for research purposes):

Deja News   http://www.dejanews.com.

Reference.com   http://www.reference.com.

To find ListServs or newsgroups by subject:

CataList: the Official Catalog of Listserv Lists
http://www.listserv.net/lists/listref.html

Liszt Directories   http://www.liszt.com.

Publicly Accessible Mailing Lists
http://www.neosoft.com/internet/paml

V. SOME INTERESTING SITES FOR RESEARCH

Environment   http://envirolink.org   http://www.earthwatch.org

FAIR (Fairness and Accuracy in Reporting)   http://www.fair.org

Federal Information Network   http://www.fedworld.gov

Humanities Research   http://humanitas.ucsb.edu/

JobWeb. job listings   http://www.jobweb.com

Library of Congress   http://lcweb.loc.gov

Literary Locales   http://www.sjsu.edu/depts/english

National Public Radio   http://www.npr.org.

New York Public Library   http://www.nypl.org.

Public Broadcasting System   http://www.pbs.org.

Smithsonian Institution   http://www.si.edu

WebMuseum   http://www.netspot.unisa.edu.at/wm/

World Lecture Hall   http://www.utexas/world/lecture/
(faculty Web sites, organized by discipline)

VI. UNUSUAL SOURCES

The sources in this list do not fit easily into any category, but they can provide some amazing information, and they're fun to browse. Check some of these sources to find an anecdote or an unusual fact to spark up your paper.

Adams, Cecil. *The Straight Dope Tells All.* New York: Ballantine, 1998. Provides answers to odd questions, such as how many square inches of skin are on the average human body. Some material is available on the Internet, http://www.straightdope.com

Benet, William Rose, and Bruce Murphy, eds. *Benet's Reader's Encyclopedia.* 4th ed. New York: HarperCollins, 1996. An encyclopedia of world literature.

Bragonia, Reginald, Jr., and David Fisher. *What's What: A Visual Glossary*. New York: Ballantine, 1981. Illustrates and names the parts of common objects.

Burnam, Tom. *Dictionary of Misinformation: The Book to Set the Record Straight*. New York: HarperCollins, 1986.

Ciardi, John. *A Browser's Dictionary: A Compendium of Curious Expressions and Intriguing Facts*. 2nd ed. New York: Harper & Row, 1983.

Feldman, David. *Imponderables: The Solution to the Mysteries of Everyday Life*. New York: Wm. Morrow & Co., 1987. First of a series, organized by questions and answers, but with index. The latest is *How Do Astronauts Scratch an Itch?* New York: Berkley, 1997.

Fried, Stephen B., and G. Ann Schultis. *The Best Self-Help and Self Awareness Books: A Topic by Topic Guide to Quality Information*. Chicago: American Library, 1995.

Grund, Bernard. *Timetables of History*. 3rd ed. New York: Simon, 1991. A horizontal depiction, in timeline style, of simultaneous historical, political, and cultural events.

Guinness Book of World Records. New York: Bantam (updated each year). Also look for Guinness books on records in aircraft, olympics, and sports.

Jones, Judy, and William Wilson. *An Incomplete Education*. New York: Ballantine, 1995. Provides a variety of information not easily found, such as explanations of the job titles in film production credits.

Kane, Joseph Nathan, Steven Anzouin, and Janet Podell. *Famous First Facts: A Record of First Happenings, Discoveries, and Inventions in American History*. New York: Wilson, 1997.

Lapham, Lewis, Michael Pollan, and Eric Etheridge. *Harper's Index Book*. New York: Holt, 1987. See also individual issues of *Harper's* magazine since 1986. Provides statistics with social and political implications, such as the number of millionaires on different presidents' cabinets.

Manguele, Alberto, and Gianni Guadalupe. *Dictionary of Imaginary Places*. San Diego: Harcourt, 1987. Catalogs and describes literary and other imaginary places from Oz to Utopia and beyond.

Mills, Jerry Leath, and Louis D. Rubin, eds. *A Writer's Companion: A Handy Compendium of Useful but Hard-to-Find Information on History, Literature, Art, Science, Travel, Philosophy, and Much More*. New York: HarperCollins, 1997.

Panati, Charles. *Extraordinary Origins of Everyday Things*. New York: Harper, 1987. Inventions of common objects.

Wiener, Philip P., ed. *Dictionary of the History of Ideas*. New York: Scribner's, 1980.

INDEX

ABOUT THE AUTHORS

A graduate of Amherst College and the University of Virginia, **Jay Silverman** has received fellowships from the Fulbright-Hayes Foundation, the Andrew Mellon Foundation, and the National Endowment for the Humanities. He has taught at Virginia Highlands Community College and at Nassau Community College where he received the Honors Program Award for Excellence in Teaching and where he also teaches in the College Bound Program of the Nassau County Mental Health Association.

Elaine Hughes came to New York City from Mississippi in 1979 to attend a National Endowment for the Humanities seminar at Columbia University. She has taught writing for more than twenty-five years—primarily at Hinds Community College in Raymond, Mississippi, and at Nassau Community College. Since her retirement from NCC and her return to Mississippi, she has conducted many writing workshops for the Esalen Institute and for other organizations. She is also the author of *Writing from the Inner Shelf.*

As Chair of the English Department of Nassau Community College for six years, **Diana Roberts Wienbroer** coordinated a department of 150 faculty members and served on the Executive Council of the Association of Departments of English. Besides teaching writing for over thirty years, both in Texas and New York, she has studied and taught film criticism. She is also the author of *The McGraw-Hill Guide to Electronic Research and Documentation*, 1997.

The authors have also written *Rules of Thumb*, 4th ed., and *Good Measures: A Practice Book to Accompany Rules of Thumb*, both available from McGraw-Hill.